MEN DANCING

Alexander Bland and John Percival

Men Dancing

Performers and Performances

Macmillan Publishing Company

New York

Picture credits

We would like to thank all the photographers, collectors and libraries who made their pictures available to us and who so generously and patiently let us keep them for so long. Their work appears on the following pages:

116, 117 Gilbert Adams (117 courtesy Dame Alicia Markova Collection); 42 left, 77, 122 left and right, 123, 124 Gordon Antony (courtesy Theatre Museum, London); 13 right, 20 top, 43 bottom, 102 left, 108, 111, 115, 120, 121, 126 BBC Hulton Picture Library; 12 right, 109 right, 107, 109 left Bibliotheque et Musée de l Opéra, Paris; 37 left Martin Bleckman; 164 Clive Boursnell; 163 top right Steven Caras; 68, 69, 88 Daniel Candé; 12 left courtesy Clark/Crisp collection; 95 Nobby Clark; 25 Andrew Cockrill; 5, 21 bottom, 65 left, 127, 154, 175 Anthony Crickmay; 153 Alan Cunliffe; 22 top right, 35 top right, 43 top, 44, 75, 76 left, 79, 100, 102 right, 103, 104, 105 Dance Collection, the New York Public Library at Lincoln Centre, Library and Museum of the Performing Arts; 31 Danish Theatre Museum; 26 top left, 41, 54, 90 right, 140 © Mike Davis Studios Ltd; 2–3, 6, 26 bottom, 45 left, 85, 87, 93, 94 left, 145 bottom, 158 Zoë Dominic; 13 left, 20 bottom Collection Parmenia Migel Ekstrom; 150 right Claire Falcy; 78 top, 134 left, 143 Fred Fehl; 30 courtesy Ivor Guest; 11 Harvard Theatre Collection; 80 Kobal Collection; 9 Jean-Dominique Lajoux; 38, 39, 40 right, 72 courtesy Lazzarini collection; 62 Janet Levitt; 23 top centre, 22 top left, 70, 71 left Serge Lido; 42 right George Platt Lynes; 40 left, 114 courtesy Nesta Macdonald; 78 bottom Angus McBean; 8, 10, 174 Mansell Collection; 55 right Colette Masson; 36 left Normand Maxon; 128 Duncan Melvin (courtesy Theatre Museum, London); 165 Herb Migdoll; 49, 58, 71 right, 152 Mira; 147 Jack Mitchell; 35 top left Barbara Morgan; 113 Museum of Modern Art/Film Stills Archive; 45 right, 89, 134 right © Mydtskov; 81, 112 National Film Archive; 21 top, 61 bottom, 73, 150 left Novosti Press Agency; 48, 60, 136, 144 bottom, 166 bottom left Louis Peres; 141, 144 top Michael Peto (courtesy Dundee University Library); 148, 151 © Roger Pic; 23 bottom William Reilly; 50 Houston Rogers (courtesy Theatre Museum, London); 146 Anne Séchaud; 46–7, 149 Society for Cultural Relations; 84, 90 left Donald Southern; 22 bottom, 27 top, 59 left and right, 155 bottom, 157, 159, 168, 172 Leslie Spatt; 173 David Street; 19 bottom, 24 bottom right, 26 top right, 33, 35 bottom, 52, 56, 63, 65 right, 66, 67 left and right, 83, 133, 135, 137, 138, 139, 160, 161, 162, 163 top left, 163 bottom, 166 top and bottom right, 167, 174 © Martha Swope; 18, 24 top left and right, and bottom left, 118 Theatre Museum, London; 23 top left, 24 bottom centre, 92, 171 © Jack Vartoogian; 55 left © Linda Vartoogian; 76 right, 99, 119, 129, 142 Roget Viollet; 36 right © Max Waldman; 19 top, 51, 91 Jennie Walton; 37 right Barbara Walz; 97, 101, 106, 130, 131 Weidenfeld & Nicolson archives; 1, 27 bottom, 53, 61 top, 64, 86, 94 right, 155 top, 169, 170 Rosemary Winckley.

Macmillan Publishing Company
866 Third Avenue, New York, N.Y. 10022

Library of Congress Cataloging in Publication Data
Bland, Alexander, and Percival, John
    Men Dancing
    Includes index.
    1. Men dancers – Biography. I. Title.
GV1785.A1B574   793.3′2′0922 [B]   82–6562
                                          AACR2

ISBN 0-02-511450-6

Designed by Simon Bell

First American edition 1984

First published in Great Britain by
George Weidenfeld and Nicolson Limited
91 Clapham High Street, London SW4 7TA

Printed in Italy

Publishers' note

Nigel Gosling's writing on dance appeared under the pen-name of Alexander Bland. When he died in 1982 after a lengthy illness, this book was left at a stage where it seemed a tragic waste to abandon it. So we were extremely fortunate that John Percival agreed to take on the difficult task of finishing a project in which he had had no hand in the planning. We are deeply grateful to him. The contents page opposite lists the authorship of the various elements in the book. The piece on Rudolf Nureyev is a posthumous compilation of material that Nigel Gosling had written over the years and we are grateful to his estate and to London Editions for allowing us to quote from *The Nureyev Image* and *An Illustrated History of Ballet and Dance* respectively. We are also grateful to Richard Buckle for contributing a foreword which conveys an idea of why Nigel Gosling is so acutely missed. But all along we have had the invaluable advice and active assistance of Maude Gosling. The book's existence owes most to her.

Nigel Gosling invented this book, planned its purpose, content and shape, and wrote a great part of it in versions ranging from rough drafts to finished copy. My function has been only to try, with his wife Maude and his devoted editor Tristram Holland, to complete it as nearly as could be to his intentions, from admiration and affection for a cherished colleague. For me, this is still Nigel's book.   *John Percival*

Half title page: Gary Chryst as the Chinese Conjurer in *Parade*, one of the many standard or created character roles in which he made his name with the Joffrey Ballet.

Title page: Dancers of the Royal Ballet in *Dances of Albion*.

Opposite: Patrick Harding-Irmer in *Chamber Dances*, one of his roles with London Contemporary Dance Theatre.

CONTENTS

FOREWORD
BY RICHARD BUCKLE

Since Nigel Gosling died while he was working on this book, so that it had to be completed by a former colleague, and since it is consequently the last of a distinguished series of works appearing under his own name or under the pen-name of Alexander Bland, readers may excuse – may perhaps even welcome – a purely personal note about an author whose worth was only equalled by his modest self-effacement.

Nigel's education at Eton and at King's College, Cambridge, followed by a spell in the Diplomatic Corps as an attaché in Berlin, can hardly account for the width of his interest in the arts: but his devotion to ballet – which drove him to take classes in classical dancing, just as he had previously worked at writing and painting – dates from his falling in love with Maude Lloyd, the beautiful South African-born ballerina of the Ballet Rambert, whom he married in 1939. When war came it was singularly audacious of Nigel, as a soldier's son, to express his conviction of its futility by declaring himself a Conscientious Objector and joining the Red Cross, with which he served at home and abroad.

It would seem that from childhood Nigel had his own quiet conviction of what was right and wrong, an individual code of behaviour. When he died, David Astor, who had been at school with him, wrote to Maude, 'I have always thought of Nigel as having a sort of perfection about him – while being modest and self-mocking at the same time. He had a kind of self-respect which made him unable to debase or compromise himself . . . He was a boy of about twelve when I first knew him. Even at that shaky age, he had a lightly-carried dignity which seemed to make him fully the equal of the adults in authority. It wasn't that he ever sought authority, which he conspicuously didn't. It was rather that he had his own ideas and lived by them.'

The friend who wrote these lines was Editor of the *Observer* from 1948 to 1975, and Nigel Gosling joined this paper as Features Editor in 1950. I was the *Observer*'s ballet critic, but it was in my capacity as editor of the little monthly magazine *Ballet* that I had recently invited Nigel and Maude to put their heads together (not that these charming receptacles were ever very far apart) and write critical essays on the dance. They were reluctant at first, and Maude doubted the propriety of her criticizing former colleagues: but they were finally persuaded.

In 1954 Nigel took over my ballet column in the *Observer*, and from 1962 to 1975 he was both the paper's art critic as well as their ballet critic. It was inevitable, therefore, as his books began to appear, that some, such as *Gustave Doré* and *Nadar*, should be about the visual arts, while others, *The Dancer's World*, *An Illustrated History of Dance and Ballet*, *The Nureyev Image*, *Fonteyn and Nureyev* and *The Royal Ballet: the first 50 years*, should be about dance. *Leningrad* and *Paris 1900–1914: The Miraculous Years* contrived to cover both subjects. He had a gift for the memorable phrase. I recall his short appreciation of a special English team spirit in the Royal Ballet. 'The Company presents a seamless closely-woven texture reminiscent of fine linen, a unanimity of purpose like that which steers a flock of wheeling birds'. Valuable and successful as his books may have been, Nigel talked and behaved as if nothing he had been or done or written was of the slightest consequence. This characteristic is what used to be called 'gentlemanly'; and indeed that forbidden word came into my mind when I watched his simple, direct and startlingly effective introduction to a television film on Nureyev.

After Nicholas, the son of Maude and Nigel Gosling, had married and made a home apart, it happened that fate in the form of Margot Fonteyn presented them with another son to adopt. When Rudolf Nureyev decided to move west she asked the Goslings to keep an eye on him. They undertook this mission so whole-heartedly that the itinerant exile came more and more frequently to shelter under their roof. They were Rudolf's best friends in the West, and he became the son of their late middle-age. If all the steaks Maude cooked for the young Russian could reassume taurine form, the resultant herd would overcrowd Hyde Park. Of Nureyev's special qualities as a dancer and choreographer nobody wrote more warmly, more perceptively or more untiringly than Nigel.

When Nigel died, Terence Kilmartin, who had worked for thirty years alongside him on the *Observer*, wrote in that newspaper: 'Nigel Gosling was so innocent of the resentments, snobberies, aggressions and neuroses that most of us are prone to that one was tempted to regard him as a sort of saint. It was not a designation that he himself – with his Puckish irreverence – would have allowed, or even understood. His gentleness and serenity were innate and instinctual. He would not have been aware that he was a man of unusual virtue as well as unusual gifts; but he was'.

Both the Goslings' post-war homes were near to Hyde Park: and I remember Nigel remarking on how agreeable it was to be able to drive all the way to the *Observer* and back through trees. That umbrageous route along the South side of Hyde Park, down Constitution Hill and along the Embankment, was frequently followed, eastwards or westwards, four times a day; because, more often than not, he came home to luncheon and to Maude.

Opposite: Rudolf Nureyev in *Vivace*, a solo created for him by Murray Louis.

The Masculine Tradition

If architecture is the 'Mother of the Arts', then dance must be their grandmother, for it was already flourishing when our ancestors were still content to use ready-mades for shelter – caves and clearings in which they stamped and bobbed and grunted in their primitive rituals. These occasions, demonstrations of group homogeneity and invocations to invisible powers, usually seem to have been sexually indiscriminating. But human instinct probably divided men from women at certain moments, giving

Battles and hunting are frequent themes in the dances of Australian Aborigines (left), which have been passed on, usually from uncle to nephew, since time immemorial.

This cave painting (below), discovered at Tassili N'Ager in the Sahara, dates from prehistoric times. One of the earliest surviving representations of men dancing, the scene bears comparison with Zulu war dances today.

special prominence – and so special dance movements – to selected individuals. These were usually men, one reason being that the athletic male body is best equipped for the violent activities thought to be needed to attract human or divine attention. In the oldest of arts, men held first place.

This evident truth is worth re-stating because, although male dancers now reign supreme, they have not always done so. Comparatively recently, the rule was broken for a spell, and the aftermath can still be felt today. During that time, the male dancer was consistently overshadowed by his female partner. This applied only to theatrical dancing – in social dances the sexes moved towards ever greater equality, and the process continues, as a visit to any popular dance hall will show. Nor was it a universal trend: in the East, where dance retains its links with religion, it has never become associated with any one gender. But in

Europe social changes brought new theatrical attitudes. The rise of capitalism in the seventeenth century led to a great expansion of display-dancing as a form of conspicuous expenditure; it became purely hedonistic, offering a variety of attractions among which sexual stimulation ranked high. Female charms became a potent ingredient.

Three hundred years later the process was complete. Dance had divorced itself from ritual, either religious or temporal, and was now mere entertainment. By the middle of the nineteenth century, dance, once a male domain, had become a 'female art' in which the participation of men seemed hardly necessary, and even unnatural. Even the title used for a male dancer, 'ballerino', virtually dropped out of use (today it survives only in Italy).

This dramatic change, which replaced the great male stars of the seventeenth and eighteenth centuries with internationally adored ballerinas, happened very suddenly, primarily because of the influence of the Romantic movement on the arts. It lasted over a hundred years and then, with equal suddenness, the old balance was restored. Today the male dancer is back in the limelight, emerging like a planet reappearing after a long eclipse – served by choreographers, acclaimed by critics and – as theatre managements can testify – outstripping his female rivals as a magnet for the public. The effeminate image of dance has vanished. On the contrary, the remote and ethereal heroine who used to be idolized by a select elite has been replaced by popular heroes as widely worshipped as film stars, tennis champions or football celebrities.

The course of male prestige in ballet shows a clear pattern – a curve which begins near the top, starts to wobble, then drops suddenly, only to shoot up again intermittently in the early years of this century, and decisively in the last twenty years. At first, men were almost unchallenged in dance. The satyrs of the Greek classical drama would not have been outshone even by the circling chorus of long-skirted maenads. In Roman times the entertainments organized for imperial and public enjoyment certainly offered crude delights from dancing girls; but male performers were far more widely acclaimed. The first two dancers whose names have come down to us were both men – the stately Pylades and the lively Bathyllus – and under Augustus the fans of rival male performers had to be restrained by law from rioting in the streets.

Such extravagances died out in the Dark Ages, but men held their own in the more modest junketings in the medieval town square or castle hall. The unwieldy robes and towering head-dresses of the women prevented them from joining in the skipping and tumbling of their companions.

The proud warlike carriage of these Roman gladiators contrasts interestingly with their graceful arms as they perform a Pyrrhic dance on a frieze from Palestrina.

Daniel Rabel's designs for men taking part in a *Ballet d'Entrée* at the Louvre, Paris, in 1625, were intended to show off the (probably professional) dancers' skills.

The profound changes in social customs introduced by the Renaissance in Italy served at first only to enhance the role of the male. The juggling and acrobatics which provided a contrast to the solemn sung and spoken episodes in the lavish diversions provided at the ducal courts were clearly masculine activities. When France emerged as a great power in the sixteenth century and their court in Paris took over these festivities, developing them into opera-ballets, men became even more prominent as symbols of a completely male-dominated society. The monarchs themselves led the dancing: Louis XIV was so keen that he took lessons almost every day. In the Grand Ballet which formed the climax to every *Ballet de Cour* – an episode in which only the nobility took part – the sexes were strictly segregated: while duchesses and countesses might perform with the Queen, only men could appear with the King. Even female roles were taken by men – a deception easy to effect since all the performers were masked and wore elaborately concealing costumes. Louis XIV himself could apparently be picked out only by a ribbon worn on his sleeve.

These stately affairs differed sharply from the lively *Ballets d'Entrée* to which professionals were soon introduced in character roles. The contrast between these and the formal grandeur of the aristocracy was marked. Virtuoso effects and comedy were left to the professionals, while Louis himself – especially in his roles as Apollo or the Sun King – became the epitome of the *danseur noble*, an image which was to leave its mark on all subsequent classical ballet.

A design by Jean Bérain for a grotesque dancer, for a ballet of the late 17th-century.

The supremacy of the male seemed at its peak; women were mere display objects, loaded with ornament and costly materials which rendered them almost immobile. But change was in the air. The range and popularity of ballet was spreading, and in 1672 the King appointed an Italian dancer, Lully (or Lulli) to set up an Academy for professional performances. At first only men were included but soon women were also admitted and in 1713 a school was set up by the Opéra, supervised by the talented Pierre Beauchamp, to train ten dancers of each sex.

A crack had appeared in male supremacy and it widened quickly and inexorably. With the accession of Louis XV the Rococo Age began and a breath of light frivolity blew through ballet. The emergence of two dramatically rival ballerinas, Marie Sallé and the delightful Marie Camargo, diverted attention even from the handsome Louis Dupré (known as 'Le Grand' on account of his height and majestic style). Camargo went so far as to challenge masculine virtuosity, daringly shortening her dress a few inches to show her ankles and thus reveal her agility, which was equalled by that of a brilliant and fascinating Italian ballerina, La Barberina. For twenty years the male dancers, though nominally taking first place, found themselves rivalled by feminine charms.

But the eighteenth-century career of the ballerina was

short and they were soon forgotten with the emergence of the mighty Gaetano Vestris, an Italian-born dancer who took Paris by storm with his elegance, good looks, noble style and overpowering presence. Nicknamed, the 'god of the dance' he ruled over ballet like an absolute monarch, fighting off the dramatic Marie-Madeleine Guimard and a rival male dancer, Charles Le Picq. Vestris would yield only to his son Auguste, who was to become even more celebrated in a different, more acrobatic, style. Famous in most of the opera houses in Europe, they were the first real international stars of ballet. When father and son danced together in London in 1781, Parliament was interrupted so that members could watch them.

During the difficult years of the Revolution, Pierre Gardel, a fine dancer in the old style, continued to defend the dignity of masculine dancing. But another revolution was in the air. In the first quarter of the nineteenth century the Romantic Movement hit the dance theatre, making it the home of dreams and fantasy. The masculine virtues of dignity, fortitude and gruff comedy were obliterated in the mists of democratic sentiment, together with the traditional conventions of rank. Women were no longer

During the 18th-century, the wide skirt – an echo of ancient Roman uniforms – became shorter and lighter allowing greater freedom of movement.

Pierre Gardel represents the old school of noble style
in his own ballet *Télémaque* at the Paris Opéra in 1790.

The ballerina comes into first place: Henri Desplaces
lifts Adèle Dumilâtre in *Le Corsaire* (1844).

chattels for masculine enjoyment; they had become lofty, elusive, often disturbing visions, to be handled by men gingerly and with respect. To cap everything, as often happens in the arts, a technical invention brought a fundamental change. The introduction of the strengthened toe-shoe in the first decade of the nineteenth century lent to the ballerinas a lightness and softness which was as theatrically effective as male athleticism. Men became mere attendants, sturdy but dull, perambulating pedestals for the display of the ballerinas' charms.

The new fashion resulted in the eclipse of male dancing for a hundred years. Technical standards did not decline, and the Opéra school turned out artists of the calibre of Jules Perrot and the Petipa brothers. But, with daintiness and prettiness permeating most of the productions, ballet itself acquired the feminine aura which haunted it until very recently.

The reign of the ballerinas came to an end almost as suddenly as it had begun, attacked from an unexpected quarter. By the end of the century ballet had declined in its traditional homes – France, Italy and England – into mere commercialized frivolity, patronized only by music-hall audiences. But in Russia, culturally always lagging behind the rest of Europe, the old values persisted. Male dancers were still taken seriously. Local talent had been fostered by a succession of teachers and choreographers imported from abroad and there was a healthy tradition of athletic folk-dancers employed to fill out the ranks of provincial companies. Male dancing was flourishing in St Petersburg and Moscow, and in 1909 it was abruptly revealed to the West by the arrival in Paris of Serge Diaghilev and his Ballets Russes company. This boasted not only ballerinas like Pavlova and Karsavina but a whole team of men of outstanding talent, avidly displayed by an openly homosexual director. The savage virility of Mordkin and Bolm injected red blood into the now anaemic veins of Western ballet, while the exotic allure of Nijinsky spread over the image of male dancing an arresting – if somewhat ambiguous – glamour.

Men were once again back in the centre of the stage. Indeed, the impact of Nijinsky was so strong that he became the very embodiment of dance – a position symbolized by his appearance (admittedly in a very androgynous pose) on the poster advertising the company. This was the first occasion on which the image of a male dancer had been used for publicity purposes – an experiment not to be repeated for fifty years. But during the whole twenty-five years of Diaghilev's activity men dominated the scene. After Nijinsky came Léonide Massine, after Massine Serge Lifar, and after Lifar Anton Dolin. Diaghilev had many charming, gifted ballerinas, but it was a man for whom Balanchine wrote his first enduring ballets, *Apollo* (1928) and *The Prodigal Son* (1929), and when Diaghilev died soon afterwards, male dancing seemed to be re-established as firmly as it had been in the seventeenth and eighteenth centuries.

But the audience for the Ballets Russes was as small as it was select. For the general public, the image of ballet as an art of gauzy skirts, feminine glamour and male nonentity still persisted, as the popularity of Pavlova in the face of all Diaghilev's resources attested. For some years after Diaghilev's death the reputation of his male stars endured, dominating the companies which arose in his wake – Dolin at Sadler's Wells, Lifar at the Paris Opéra, Massine with Colonel de Basil's Russian Ballet, Bolm and Mordkin in America. But nobody emerged to replace them and it was women who led the younger generation – Darsonval and Chauviré in Paris, Markova and Fonteyn in London, Danilova in America and the immensely popular 'baby ballerinas' introduced by de Basil. By the mid-1930s, the brief revival of the male dancer seemed to be over – so much so that Balanchine was now driven to declare that 'ballet belongs to women'.

Once again it was the Russians who changed the picture in favour of men. A virile tradition had continued there, led by the Bolshoi Ballet in Moscow with its heroic stars, and the nobly elegant men in the Kirov Ballet in Leningrad. When they appeared in the West, audiences were stunned by the standard of their men – correct and skilled, but dramatic, strong and assertive; able to hold their own with fine dancers like Ulanova and Kolpakova. By comparison, their Western counterparts seemed unassertive; even a distinguished star like the Danish Erik Bruhn remained a specialist attraction.

In Russia, at least, male dancing was manifestly flourishing. Then, a single unexpected event changed the whole picture in the West, too, tipping the balance decisively in favour of the men. In 1961 the most promising young male dancer in the Kirov Ballet, Rudolf Nureyev, stayed in the West after a triumphant season with the company in Paris. This dramatic debut was followed by equally successful appearances in London and New York and almost immediately he became the biggest attraction in the ballet world, with a personality on and off-stage which spread his fame far outside dance circles. The reaction was far-reaching. Ballet itself reached new audiences and male dancers in particular found themselves the centre of attention. The 'Nijinsky phenomenon' had worked again.

The impact was to prove more durable this time round, if only because Nureyev's range was wider, his appearances more frequent and more international and his career much longer. Even so, the shock might have worn off with time if he had not been followed to the West ten years later by another outstanding Kirov dancer, Mikhail Baryshnikov. Once again, it was a male dancer who made headlines in the newspapers and attracted queues outside theatres. In a single generation men won back their honourable status and in so doing added strength, solidity and breadth to an art always on the brink of dwindling into specialized or trivial charm. The effeminate, élitist image of dance has disappeared – the new heroes are followed by a public as large and as diverse as that of any other entertainment star.

This revolution is manifestly rooted in general cultural and social changes, for it is visible also in films and straight theatre, where men have largely replaced women as major box-office attractions. But it can also be ascribed to one or two individuals. What Taglioni and Elssler did for the ballerina in the nineteenth century, Nureyev and Baryshnikov have achieved for the male dancer in the twentieth. Exciting new dancers seem to emerge everywhere; the strong difference between their styles and temperaments has served to fan the flames of rivalry among their admirers and an upsurge of interest and talent has sprung up around them. Once again men appear on the posters – this time flaunting their masculinity; choreographers devise ballets for them; schoolboys are fired by the ambition to win fame and fortune (for they are now as well paid as the ballerinas) as dancers. In this new atmosphere we can look again at the great male artists of the past and examine their achievements alongside those of their counterparts today.

Classical Pedigree and Dramatic Heritage

t may be rash but it is not unjustified to divide dancers – including male dancers – into different groups like singers. Critics are often accused of killing their victims by dissecting them and there is some truth in the charge. Art is part of life and so indivisible; every manifestation of it is unique and immune to analysis. But understanding depends on generalization and for practical reasons it is useful to codify. Dance has been about the last form of human expression to be laid out on the operating table, mainly because it was, until recently, impossible to record it. But now we can squarely face the obligation to submit it to classification and comparison.

Male singers were so divided – into tenors, baritones and basses – as early as the sixteenth century. The same kind of grouping must have prevailed in dance since the earliest times: the leaping satyr in a Greek drama would hardly have been the same performer chosen to play the hero (or heroine). Similar influences – mostly physical – operate today. Some of them are easy to understand – a stocky dynamic dancer would not fit naturally into the role of a dignified nobleman. But others are more mysterious. Individual temperament is important: the style of a choreographer can mould that of the dancers for whom he composes; and sometimes social or even racial characteristics seem to play a part.

Nature itself separates one dancer from another, but few troupes today can support specialist performers. In addition, modern choreographers demand increasing versatility from their artists. For these and other reasons the different types have slowly become confused and overlapping. Top performers are expected – and indeed themselves expect – to excel in every field, sometimes even to duplicate the movement of the opposite sex. A dancer who is the counterpart of a lyrical tenor may find himself in a role suited to a heroic baritone, or vice versa. This can produce unjust comparisons, confused assessments and mistaken ambitions. The dancer of today has a wide range; except in rare cases, his basic natural aptitude is always discernible. Analysis can only help us to admire when it is overcome, to rejoice when it is fully exploited and extended.

Dancers began to be classified in the rational climate which developed in Italy with the birth of the Renaissance. As early as 1416 a certain Domenico di Piacenza was listing the different qualities expected of them – grace, agility, control and the ability to 'undulate like a gondola'. One of his pupils, Guglielmo Ebreo, a famous ballet-master, wrote down his own definitions a generation later, in 1463; they included a sense of rhythm, a feeling for space, lightness and gracefulness, an accurate memory, style, temperament and plasticity. These were general recommendations applicable to all dancers; he was writing for amateur performers executing variations on the normal ballroom steps of the time. But the foundations of technical analysis had been laid. Italy was the birthplace of the intellectual approach to dance.

With the rise of France in the sixteenth century the Paris court inherited the whole paraphernalia of formal dancing, including the typically Renaissance list of suitable subject matter – heroic or symbolic – and the conception of a formal hierarchy among the performers. Italian musicians and ballet-masters reigned in Paris. It was for one of them, Jean Baptiste Lully (earlier known as Giambattista Lulli) that Louis set up the Académie Royale de Musique in 1672. There the French teacher Pierre Beauchamp is credited with establishing ballet's five basic positions of the feet. A similar classification of the dancers themselves into the three fundamental categories, or genres, probably stems also from this time, although it was not specifically recorded in print.

The demarcation lines were jealously guarded by later ballet-masters such as Louis Dupré, Gaetano Vestris and Pierre Gardel, all renowned as dancers and teachers of strict academic correctitude. The classifications were clearly set down at last in 1760 by the choreographer Jean-Georges Noverre in his book *Letters on the Dance*. He divided male dancers into three types – the Serious or Heroic, the Semi-serious or Demi-caractère, and the Comic or Grotesque. In the manner of his age the styles carried degrees of prestige, a system of artistic (and sometimes pecuniary) preference which was to last for generations.

First stood the Serious dancer or *danseur noble*: he descends from Renaissance princes, Roman heroes and, further back still, from the gods and kings and awe-inspiring figures who represented – or sometimes actually embodied – divine power. Louis XIV himself (an enthusiastic dancer) provided the archetypal model. Noverre laid down that he should be of 'a noble and elegant stature' (that is, tall), with 'fine features and a proud bearing', and he should 'bear the mark of tragedy': he must possess that *gravitas* which separates the tragic from the merely pathetic. Mimicking is not for him. He has to convey a sense of authority and strength through his presence, stance, walk, gestures and even his way of sitting. A graceful line, correct technique and harmonious movement are obligatory, but not enough in themselves, while nimble acrobatics would be actually out of place.

This lofty ideal soon began to slip as elements of show-off virtuosity crept in. Noverre himself complained that 'the practice introduced by dancers of employing cabrioles in the noble style of dancing has altered the character and deprived it of dignity'. Sixty years later the Milanese ballet-master Carlo Blasis was equally severe about the proper separation of the categories: 'Nothing reveals a lack of taste in a dancer more strongly than the choice of a style which does not correspond to his capabilities. The mixture of several branches of his art in a single person is to be deplored.' He blamed contemporary attempts at versatility on inexpert audiences and on performers of minor talent imitating a dancer of genius. 'I would be happy that he who has the stature, the aptitudes and the technique which distinguish Monsieur [Auguste] Vestris, should tackle all kinds of role; but let him who is endowed with a generous physique confine himself to the Serious style, while he who has a modest stature should stick to Demi-caractère work with acrobatic steps, or to the romantic style.'

Following academic practice, Blasis also recognized the three categories – Serious, Demi-caractère and Comic or Rustic. He insisted on physical aptitude; only those built like Apollo or Antinous are deemed suitable for the Serious style. They must be tall of course, with 'perfectly proportioned legs, neat ankles and great ease and flexibility in the hips'. They should have 'an elegant and distinguished bearing, full of grace and dignity but free of all affectation'. Blasis admits that the Serious range is limited, but he places it at the top of his scale: 'The Serious genre is the most difficult . . . The proper execution of an adagio variation is the summit of our art.' He declared that he knew only one dancer capable of excelling in it.

To this majestic figure, the second category – the Demi-caractère or Semi-serious dancer – served as light relief: vigorous, skilled and charming. According to Noverre, he should be of medium height, slim and elegant, with 'the proportions of Canova's Mercury'; his attack should be imbued with restraint and 'a certain attractive dignity'. Requiring 'less fine features, but an agreeable and attractive bearing', he is marked by 'the dignity of the upper part of his body, by the harmonious combination of his movements and by the perfect finish of his dancing.' We can conclude that, like many dancers today, he was Classical down to the waist, while his legs and feet betrayed a certain friskiness.

Visibly descended from the trained professionals who supported the aristocratic amateurs of the Court ballets, this type of artist, with his freedom and agility and his roots in a lyrical and dramatic tradition, was clearly the best equipped for the future development of ballet. The workings of evolution put a premium on flexibility; while the pure Classical dancer was perhaps doomed to suffer the fate of the sabre-toothed tiger – once the king of the jungle – the humbler breed of mixed-type artist flourished more and more. We can recognize in Noverre's description of the Demi-caractère artist most of today's male dancers: they have even begun to usurp the label 'Classical'. In America, for instance, the choreography of Balanchine has developed a Demi-caractère style, close to that of Bournonville-trained dancers, which has become almost the local dialect of the Classical tradition.

The stern classification established two hundred years ago can be traced in practice right through the nineteenth century – with Auguste Vestris stepping in during the first decades to establish the supreme model of the Demi-caractère dancer, as his father Gaetano had set the standard for pure Classicism, and Jules Perrot succeeding him as an outstanding artist in the same genre; less talented artists like Louis Mérante continued to uphold male dignity during these Dark Ages for the male dancer. The line was never broken – though it faltered in the West after the arrival of Diaghilev who, engrossed in the experiments of his young choreographers, was not at first interested in traditional Classicism; for his 1921 *Sleeping Beauty* he had to import a St Petersburg dancer Pierre Vladimiroff, to play the Prince.

In our own times another great codifier, Ninette de Valois, recalled the traditional classifications with characteristic crispness in 1937, in her book *Invitation to the Ballet* – even adding some additions of her own. To the attributes of the truly Classical artist, the *danseur noble*, she ascribed the curious quality of 'lethargy' – by which she presumably meant that measured ease which gives weight and authority to a movement – slowness here becoming a virtue. She notes the sub-division of this genre which arose in the nineteenth century, the Classical-Romantic, as opposed to the Classical-Heroic, dancer. Above all, she boldly adds a whole new category to the Demi-caractère genre – the acrobatic virtuosos whom she labels Academic-Classical: 'Great facility as opposed to great talent is the general feature of these dancers, who are short in stature and generously endowed with muscular strength; they possess brilliance, speed and precision.' She adds perceptively, 'Classicism as demanded of the *danseur noble* has an innate quality; Academic Classicism a routine virtuosity more usually found in apt physical type ... The *danseur noble* is the symbol of classical form of creation, the other of classical technique or execution.'

De Valois insists again on the importance of differentiation. 'Even members of the corps de ballet ... show, from their student days to the close of their careers, the style they must adopt through the demands of their talents.' The same segregation holds good today in that stronghold of conservatism, Soviet Russia, and is even officially recognized – at least in the academic strongholds of the Kirov Ballet. 'A dancer's physical appearance, not only his technical capabilities led to his use either as a *danseur noble* or Demi-caractère', writes Gennadi Smakov in his biography of Mikhail Baryshnikov. 'Softly curving, longish "Apollonian" muscles indicated a lyrical-romantic emploi; a Herculean build with more prominent muscles would put the dancer into the heroic repertoire ... The specifications for men were strictly defined. *Danseurs nobles* must be tall, have large features, broad shoulders, long arms and a regal bearing.' An echo of the old hierarchic grading can be detected in the differentiation between them and the lighter, more entertaining, Demi-caractère heroes of works like *Don Quixote*. Small 'Grotesque' dancers are relegated to ethnic numbers, jesters or satyrs. (Incidentally, the word 'emploi' in the sense of 'category' seems to occur only in Russian ballet circles, presumably inherited from some foreign teacher.)

The Kirov pedigree is jealously guarded. Purists there are inclined to look down on the ultra-virile, muscle-bound heroes developed in Moscow and the difference in approach is still visible. It is no accident that it was at the Imperial theatre of St Petersburg that the regal tradition was best preserved. That was where the audience was most experienced and pernickety, and theirs was, after all, an aristocratic ideal. Blue blood was represented by purity of line, executive power by strength exerted with discretion, dignity by serenity, security by poise and relaxed smoothness of execution. The ability to soar like an eagle rather than dart like a swallow, to command the stage with a glance and to suggest superhuman majesty by a control

Pavel Gerdt as Prince Désiré in the first production of *The Sleeping Beauty* (1890) shows the majesty expected then as well as the romanticism more usual nowadays.

so perfect that it transmutes an artificial convention into the semblance of divine law – these were the marks of the true Classical dancer. Classicism is a matter of style, not of technique.

Like that of genuine royalty, the style of the *danseur noble* was maintained by limiting his gestures and even emotions. Though always courteous and supportive, he would not visibly excel as a lover: passion of any kind would be out of character. But, just as the diatonic musical scale was stretched by the demands of Romanticism, so ballet's heroes were compelled more and more to portray erotic ardour, ferocious or rebellious sentiment, and even private despair. Noverre would probably have placed even Albrecht, the hero of *Giselle*, in the Demi-caractère class, as 'pastoral and voluptuous'. Today we

Three studies of Albrecht in *Giselle* from some of the most beautifully pure Classical dancers of recent years.

John Gilpin (left) was the finest English male dancer of his time, unmatched for the perfect simplicity and simple perfection of his line, with a musicality to match his elegance. His career took in both Ballet Rambert and the Royal Ballet, but the company with which he danced longest was Festival Ballet, with its international tours, so he took the English style at its best to an exceptionally wide audience. The studio picture brings out the composed reticence of his Classical style but not the ardour that went with it and gave it life.

Yuri Soloviev (above, right) is luckier; the camera has captured something of his Russian emotional richness in the role, as well as his more rounded Kirov line in the expressive inclination of the head towards the raised arm, the delicate strength of his pose.

Fernando Bujones (below, right), trained partly by Russian teachers at the School of American Ballet, has something of both the others in his pose: the long line of the raised leg emphasizing elegance, the curved upper body and head thrown back to bring out the romantic feeling. All three of them illustrate the extent to which it has become possible for a man to dance with fastidious delicacy but no loss of virile power. Although quite different in looks, character and upbringing, they derive their qualities from separate currents of one strong tradition, the power of which is indicated by the statement by Peter Martins (different again in background and quality) that as a young student he was inspired by pictures of Gilpin which 'looked like splendid sculptures'.

expect our Classical hero to present a human face just as we demand of him a high degree of virtuosity, so long as it does not turn to exhibitionist dazzle. In these democratic days, he may find, too, that his once élitist qualities are disseminated. We hold now that divinity resides in all men, and an entire corps de ballet may be asked to assume the dignity once confined to those of high rank.

A few of the attributes of the *danseur noble* survive – sometimes rather anomalously. A stoney-faced anonymity may accompany movements of eye-catching dexterity previously reserved for acrobats; the strutting peacock walk may end in undignified skipping or grotesquely contorted poses; above all, the characteristic 'penguin' carriage of the arms – originally stretched wide to avoid brushing the wide skirted coats worn by the rich in the seventeenth century – is adopted for occasions and manoeuvres manifestly calling for a more natural position. The Demi-caractère dancer has taken possession of the field; though his mixed ancestry is often revealed in half-digested styles of behaviour.

He clearly encroaches today on the territory previously reserved for the blue-blooded Classical hero. But he also strays frequently – and profitably – into the world of the last of the three categories marked out by the codifiers – the Grotesque, Rustic or Comic dancer. As drama rather than ritual became the mainspring of ballet, choreographers began to draw on real life in the same way that Molière replaced Racine. The whole gamut of human behaviour came within the range of the dancer, and there was no limit either to the expressive extremes which a single character might reach, or to the combinations of behaviour which he might exhibit. A favourite dramatic device was to present one type disguised as another. A single performer could be expected to offer, in succession, examples of styles once reserved for specialists – a gavotte might be followed by an ethnic number, pathos by comedy, graceful partnering by athletic gymnastics. The scope for a Demi-caractère or Character dancer today is as wide as human nature itself and even wider – for he may embody a spirit, a reptile, a social attitude, even a machine.

But even now it is possible to identify certain basic roles which have fallen within his province since dance first began and which have, while changing, persisted. It seems likely that they are rooted in psychological needs and drives, so it is worth while trying to isolate a few of them and trace their history.

The quintessentially masculine role is that of the Warrior. In primitive societies the fighting man was the most important member of the group; he figures prominently in their rituals; he appears in different guises in every stage of dance history of every nation; and he is still active today in a variety of disguises. Identified originally with the Leader (the Warrior-King) he is given the most eye-catching dances, the most splendid costumes. He shakes his spear in prehistoric wall paintings; the Greeks identified his skill in dancing with valour in battle, and Romulus indulged in ritual war-mimes. In the Middle Ages ritualized battle moved out of doors onto the jousting field, and stylized struggles between the forces of good and evil enlivened the popular religious plays; and in the more civilized entertainments of the Renaissance, the usual male costume with its short skirt was actually an adaptation of Roman military uniform.

With the flowering of the Romantic Movement in the nineteenth century, individual struggle replaced public battles as a theatrical subject, and intriguing deviations from the original theme stem from this time. At first the Poet ousted the Warrior as an acceptable hero; but by the end of the century the fashion for medievalism restored more martial figures, such as the Crusader hero of *Raymonda*; swords (which had been relegated for a time to the music hall) flashed again before distinguished audiences.

He exactly fitted the mould of the Moscow Classical hero and is still a familiar figure in ballets like *Spartacus*. In the West today, the traditional fighting man appears mostly in archaic reconstructions, such as the Polovtsian dances in *Prince Igor*. But his features can be traced beneath a huge variety of disguises, from the athletes in Robert North's *Troy Game* or the two rivals in Robbins's *Dances at a Gathering* to the sophisticated competition of Balanchine's *Agon* (or 'Struggle'). Conflict is an essential element in most art and the Warrior, champion of his team, seems likely to survive indefinitely on the ballet stage in one guise or another.

Using the same spear, the original fighting man became the Hunter, providing for the family or group, and in this capacity appeared frequently in tribal rituals. But a Hunter presupposes a quarry and here an even richer role for the

The male dancer as warrior: Harold Turner (top) as the Red Knight in the Royal Ballet's *Checkmate* has the Black Queen (Pamela May) at his mercy.

An earlier example: Adolph Bolm (left, below) as the chief warrior in Diaghilev's Ballet's production of the Polovtsian Dances from *Prince Igor*.

The escaped slaves arm themselves (top) and prepare to fight against their oppressors in the Bolshoi Ballet's most famous modern production, *Spartacus*.

Patrick Harding-Irmer with members of London Contemporary Dance Theatre (below) in Robert North's choreographic joke about fighters and athletes, *Troy Game*.

The male dancer as bird: the best known example is probably the Bluebird from *Sleeping Beauty*; here Yuri Soloviev soars in full flight in the Kirov Ballet's version.

Ted Shawn (above, right), a pioneer of dance as a career for men in the USA, and founder of an all-male company, evokes a great eagle in this solo, but would have difficulty actually leaving the ground in that costume.

Man into beast: Alexander Grant (below), as Bottom in the Royal Ballet's *The Dream*, has been turned into an ass, and his solo makes a silly ass of him on full pointe.

Character dancer appears. The representation of animals in dance, both during invocations to success in the chase or as part of a totem ritual, is traditional; often the two roles are mysteriously linked. The peculiarities of all kinds of beasts, from the sinuous tiger to the comically grimacing monkey, have inspired performers in many cultures and their descendants survive today though often much transformed (the 'Faune' in Nijinsky's famous ballet, *L'Après midi d'un faune*, is an intriguing example).

  More rewarding for the strictly Demi-caractère dancer (especially in his Academic virtuoso aspect) are the birds who skim and soar through ballet in every century and every country. Though sometimes it is women who embody their seductive vulnerability (as in *Swan Lake*, in Fokine's *Firebird* or in certain oriental fan-dances), men often win the roles on account of their greater elevation. Their flashing elusiveness has made them obvious symbols for the spiritual world (as in Petipa's celebrated Bluebird in *The Sleeping Beauty*). They fly through many a Renaissance ballet as a symbol of joy; but they can arouse awe, as in Ted Shawn's famous Indian eagle solo, or even menace, like the owl-magician in *Swan Lake*.

The deer as a hunter's prey is a recurring theme in the dances of the native Indians throughout north, central and south America. The example above is derived from the Yagri Indian deer dance and is given by Ramon Galindo of the New York-based Ballet Hispanico.

Roland Petit (top centre) in his own ballet *Le Loup*, plays a wolf who proves more capable of gratitude than the human characters.

The Monkey King (top right) is met widely in the dance dramas of India and Indonesia, a figure of cunning, impudence and magic powers, but fundamentally good. He occurs also in the popular acrobatic theatre of China known as 'Peking Opera', where he adds airborne bravado to his skills.

The Faun is a mythical creature, but Vaslav Nijinsky's *L'Après-midi d'un faune* (danced, right, by Rudolf Nureyev) represents him vividly as a creature of languid, self-centred voluptuousness and eroticism.

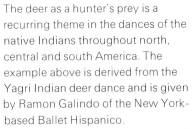

23

This bird-ogre is a variant of another male role – that of the Monster or Demon. Women seldom appear as evil – even witches are usually played by men – probably because power is an essential ingredient of the role and its dance-equivalent is strength. Decked out in terrifying but spectacular costumes, the Demon figures in almost all ethnic dances – often as the central character – and he has appeared in evil splendour in countless masques and ballets. The image changed with the centuries as a belief in magic faded. Originally ideal for a Grotesque or full Character dancer, he has gradually been humanized and made more acceptable; today he is usually either a sinister 'outsider', often personifying Death; an almost heroic figure, such as the Satan of de Valois's *Job*; or watered down to become the Victorian idea of Shakespeare's fairies such as Puck or Ariel. As such he can often be danced in Demi-caractère style.

Male dancers as demons and spirits: a prime example of a demon is Kostchei in *The Firebird*. Alexei Bulgakov, for many years leading mime of the Bolshoi Ballet, is seen here (opposite, top left) in the original Diaghilev production with the ballet's choreographer, Mikhail Fokine, as Ivan Tsarevich kneeling at his feet.

Carabosse, the wicked fairy in *The Sleeping Beauty*, has usually, though not always, been played by a man. In the original 1890 production, Enrico Cecchetti played both that role and the Bluebird. Robert Helpmann (opposite, top right) in the 1946 production at Covent Garden doubled as Carabosse and the Prince.

Anton Dolin (opposite, bottom left) was the original Satan in Ninette de Valois' *Job*, a fallen angel of demonic force and malevolence.

Demons of all sorts are found in the dances of India and the Far East. They wear either very elaborate make-up or terrifying masks like the one opposite, bottom centre, from Bhutan in the Himalayas.

A more benevolent but still capricious being endowed with magical powers is Puck in *A Midsummer Night's Dream*. Arthur Mitchell (opposite, bottom right) was his first interpreter for New York City Ballet, where Balanchine's choreography made him a sensuously exotic creature.

Another Shakespearean spirit who hovers between good and evil magic is Ariel in *The Tempest*. Wayne Eagling (right) is seen flying – with the aid of wires – in Nureyev's production for the Royal Ballet, with Anthony Dowell as Prospero.

Comedy has a wide range of possibilities for the male dancer. Michael Coleman (right) in Jerome Robbins' *The Concert* plays a husband with a roving eye who is impelled by the music to imagine himself as a butterfly, chasing a pretty girl similarly transformed.

Mikhail Baryshnikov (far right) in *Push Comes to Shove* wins laughs not from a comic characterization but by the frequent unexpected developments in the dances Twyla Tharp made for him, and in his relationship with two contrasted leading women. His hat plays a big part in the action.

Dressing up as women is often part of the fun. The comedy of the ugly sisters (bottom right) in Frederick Ashton's *Cinderella*, played here by Ashton, left, and Robert Helpmann, is based partly on the traditional English pantomime dame.

Perhaps the most direct descendants of the Roman, Renaissance and early French Character dancers are the jesters and comics who scamper and grimace and jig their way through modern ballets. Today, these descendants of the satyrs and tumblers of early entertainments have sometimes also been transmuted almost into their opposites; we may find a pathetic clown, such as Petrushka, a tender, delicate demon like Fokine's Spectre de la Rose, a tragic jester like Shakespeare's Mercutio. Fortunately the resilient spirit of comedy survives, either in watered-down versions like the jesters of Soviet ballet, or full-blooded as in Massine's Peruvian traveller in *Gaîté Parisienne*, Alain in Ashton's *La Fille mal gardée*, or the bowler-hatted joker in Twyla Tharp's *Push Comes to Shove*. There are few female comic roles; laughs are traditionally left to the men.

The most striking evidence of the extraordinary range available to the male dancer is the Travesty part, in which he is actually called upon to impersonate the opposite sex. Apart from a short period at the end of the nineteenth century when girls portrayed heroes, men have dominated the theatrical scene to such an extent that women were often debarred from appearing. Perhaps for religio-magic reasons (but more likely from psychological or social

Alexander Grant's silly suitor Alain (left) in *La Fille mal gardée* rides his umbrella like an imaginary horse.

Men as women are not always funny: Madge the fortune-telling hag in *La Sylphide* (Niels Bjørn Larsen, bottom left) exacts terrible vengeance for a small slight.

ones) they were usually excluded from primitive rituals; we find the famous Bathyllus taking female roles in ancient Rome; Shakespeare's heroines were played by boys; and in the Japanese theatre men impersonate women even today. In France young noblemen took the part of women in the Court entertainment; Louis XIV himself danced the role of a nymph in 1665 and the first professional women dancers did not appear until sixteen years later. With the development of the narrative ballet, advances in technical virtuosity and drastic changes in the social status of women, the practice of male Travesty dancing for the most part died out. But it still survives in certain strong Character roles, either comic, like the Ugly Sisters in *Cinderella*, or malignant like the witch in *La Sylphide*.

An important footnote to the subject of Travesty dancing – vital indeed to the whole subject of this book – is the fact that the levelling process which has tended to produce all-purpose dancers, has also resulted in the blurring of the distinctions between men and women (a reflection perhaps of a wider social change). Many choreographers today allot to women athletic, acrobatic movements previously considered as unfeminine. Ballerinas often dance in identical apparel to their partners and are admired as much for their strength and attack (particularly in Russia and America) as for their gentler qualities; in the same way men may be given soft, undulating movements far removed from earlier virile ideals.

Meanwhile, however, Character roles of the kind mentioned give the male dancer an advantage over his female counterpart. The whole gamut lies open to him and at some time in his career he may tackle them all; the physical changes brought by age usually mean that, as with a singer, his 'voice' tends to drop, giving him a new range or category (even virtuoso Demi-caractère stars end up as elderly Character dancers). In the same way differences in climate, physique or social conditions modulate the interpretations of the basic roles. Much has always depended on a few individual talents – but not all. They can usefully be regarded in relation to their compatriots and contemporaries.

Periods, Places and Performances

It is practically impossible even to try and list the best male dancers of the last three hundred years – the lifetime of theatrical dance in the West. Early performances were meagrely discussed and sometimes went unrecorded, and moreover, the unjust law of perspective comes into play: the dancers nearest to us in time or place loom larger than their remote predecessors or distant colleagues. Consequently only a selection of dancers must stand as representatives of their fellow-artists, but those given a place will suggest the range and achievements of male dancing yesterday and today.

One feature that emerges is the concentration of talent in certain periods and certain countries. This is a slightly mysterious phenomenon; it must arise from a mixture of social, artistic, historical and purely physical causes. That the Classical style flourishes most strongly today in East European countries is almost certainly due to the conservatism of Communist policy and public taste. On the other hand, the planting of a Classical tradition in New York by George Balanchine during the past fifty years shows the influence that a single choreographer of genius can have. Meanwhile, the fact that Russia tends to produce the dance equivalent of the baritone singer – strong, virile and broadly dramatic – while British dancers have tended to the lyrical tenor type of dancer – elegant, subtle, light and sophisticated – seems to arise from differences of build as much as background, temperament or training. One of the pleasures of modern international dance is this diversity, produced by the many influences affecting it.

Within any national tradition, some periods produce an unexpected cluster of talent. The presence of fine teachers and a strong company seem essential prerequisites for this, while the presence of one great maverick dancer of genius can inspire others to emulate and compete.

One of the earliest manifestations of this phenomenon happened in France in the early nineteenth century; the arrival of the Vestris family into a milieu where standards were already high encouraged the development of many outstanding male dancers in the next generation. More recently it has been seen at work in Denmark since the 1950s when Harald Lander, an outstanding dancer and teacher, took charge of a company with long-established traditions, inspiring a small country to produce a disproportionate number of fine dancers. More recently still, under the guidance of George Balanchine, the high standard of graduates from the School of American Ballet in New York led the great choreographer to claim with justification that corps de ballet dancers in New York City Ballet could be compared with soloists in the Diaghilev Ballet of half a century earlier. Probably the most sustained result of this kind has been seen in Russia, under the influence of some great male dancers who developed in friendly rivalry during the 1930s and became an outstanding generation of teachers and coaches.

Indeed, in any account of male dancing, Russia must stand first. A vigorous tradition of folk dance enriched the benefits derived from foreign ballet-masters such as Gaspero Angiolini, who brought Italian technique in the late eighteenth century, and Charles Didelot, who arrived from Paris in 1801 bringing French elegance with him. Jules Perrot, another Frenchman, reinforced the tradition, and Christian Johansson, a Swedish pupil of Bournonville, contributed Danish speed and dexterity. By the second half of the nineteenth century, Russian male dancers began to make their mark first in Moscow, where Vassily Geltzer's expressive character dancing was revealed in roles such as Ivanushka in *The Hump-backed Horse*, and where Sergei Sokolov was admired for his grace and lightness as well as his dramatic gifts. In St Petersburg, the French choreographer Marius Petipa (engaged in 1847 originally as a dancer) was not interested in male virtuosity and seldom bothered to compose solos for men, but during his regime Pavel Gerdt, a fine Classical partner, enjoyed a remarkably long career. Even though he was given few opportunities to shine except as a support to the ballerina, he was able to establish the precedent of beautiful line, soft arm movements and expressive flow of dance and mime that set the standard for Classical male dancers in that city. The brothers Nicolai and Sergei Legat introduced a more brilliant virtuosity in Petersburg, while Vassili Tikhomirov in Moscow, with his athletic plasticity, introduced the heroic image of the Russian Classical hero. He was followed by Mikhail Mordkin, later Pavlova's partner in the West.

In 1909 the scene was drastically changed when Diaghilev left with his company and launched the Ballets Russes in Paris. He took with him some of the finest male dancers of the new generation, notably Mikhail Fokine, Nijinsky and the character dancer Adolph Bolm. But another generation soon grew up in Leningrad under the tutelage of Vladimir Ponomaryov (himself formerly a dancer of quality). Among his pupils were Pyotr Gusev, Vakhtang Chabukiani, Konstantin Sergeyev and Alexei Yermolayev. Yermolayev revealed a powerful, virile

The double role of the explorer Lord Wilson (above) and an ancient Egyptian in *Pharaoh's Daughter* marked Marius Petipa's transition from dancer to fulltime choreographer.

cheslav Gordeyev, showed that Leningrad did not have a monopoly of romantic leading men, and dancers like Sergei Koren and Georgi Farmanyantz carried Character dancing to new levels of virtuosity.

Meanwhile, the Kirov Ballet was led for a long time by two other exceptional dancers, Konstantin Sergeyev and Vakhtang Chabukiani, representing the romantic and heroic Classical styles. They were followed by Yuri Soloviev (who rewardingly combined those qualities) and the more reserved Vladilen Semenov. However, Rudolf Nureyev's sudden departure from the Kirov in 1961, followed a few years later by the brilliant young Mikhail Baryshnikov and the outstanding Character dancer Valeri Panov, gravely weakened the company, which was further damaged by Soloviev's suicide. It is only lately that an accomplished new generation has begun to come forward. The growth of many other companies throughout the Soviet Union has provided reserves of strength; especially notable is the number of men who began their career at the school in Riga. These include Baryshnikov, and Maris Liepa and Vladimir Gelvan – two fine dancers in the romantic Classical mode now working respectively in Moscow and West Berlin.

The constant regeneration of Russian excellence is a prime example of national physical type, tall and supple, playing a part in conjunction with excellent teaching in producing outstanding male dancers. If all the Russian-born dancers scattered around the world could be brought together, they would form a team unrivalled anywhere. Overall, Russian male dancers are still the best.

The Russian pedigree stretches back to the first Italian teachers imported in the eighteenth century. Ballet really began in Italy, so it is not surprising that the first famous names belong to Italians, but during the eighteenth century they scattered around Europe: the Vestris family to France, Angiolini to Russia, as we have seen, Vicenzo Galeotti to Denmark, while Salvatore Viganò toured extensively before settling in Milan to create his 'choreo-dramas'. Later, Carlo Blasis as teacher was the real founder of the Milan school, but during the nineteenth century its ballerinas eclipsed the men, except in the case of Enrico Cecchetti. Cecchetti made a triumphant progress through European capitals before settling in St Petersburg where he created both Carabosse and Bluebird (mime and virtuoso roles respectively) in *The Sleeping Beauty*. Cecchetti's teaching helped develop many great dancers of this century, including Pavlova, but in his

quality in the classics, with exceptionally soaring leaps and dizzyingly fast turns which, together with his mastery of difficult partnering and his dramatic forcefulness, inspired Soviet choreographers to develop a new, more heroic style of ballet spectacle for him that affected all his successors. Yermolayev was transferred in 1930 to Moscow, where Asaf Messerer (another dancer of wide range) had already been embellishing male technique with multiple *tours en l'air* and other bravura techniques. Their innovations have been inherited by such dancers as Vladimir Vasiliev, the brusquely virile Mikhail Lavrovsky, the impetuous Yuri Vladimirov, and by a more recent generation, among whom Alexander Godunov was outstanding before he left Russia for the West. However, other leading dancers from Moscow's Bolshoi Ballet, including Yuri Zhdanov, Nicolai Fadeyechev and Vat-

native land the supremacy of opera has forced the best Italian dancers to work abroad. Among them, Paolo Bortoluzzi had his best roles with Béjart's company and also became a star of American Ballet Theatre; a new generation of young hopefuls has recently followed him to join companies in Britain, America and Germany.

France was the heir to Italy, and a galaxy of talent quickly emerged from the Academy founded by Lully in 1672; among them were Pierre Beauchamp, who codified ballet's classic five positions. The noble Classical style flowered in Jean Balon, Louis Dupré, Charles Le Picq and Pierre Gardel. Later, with the rise of Romanticism, Jean-Georges Noverre's advocacy of realism in ballet produced a different kind of dancer: dramatic Demi-caractère stars such as Jules Perrot, Arthur Saint-Léon and the Petipa brothers, Lucien and Marius, who were all celebrated choreographers as well as dancers. But even these were often over-shadowed by their ballerinas who took precedence at that time, and a decadent period followed.

When revival came in this century, native French

Jules Perrot, here in his *Esmeralda* with Carlotta Grisi, was noted for his lightness and agility as a dancer, and received praise equal to Taglioni's, even in *La Sylphide*.

achievements were overshadowed at first by the greater fame of Diaghilev's company which was based primarily in France, but such Classical dancers as Albert Aveline and Serge Peretti arose at the Paris Opéra. Serge Lifar, appointed ballet director at the Opéra after Diaghilev's death, developed a repertory in which other male stars could eventually rise although the fine romantic dancer Roland Petit and charismatic Jean Babilée soon broke away. However, Alexandre Kalioujny and Michel Renault led a new generation at the Opéra, since when an almost embarrassingly rich collection of talent has appeared there. All have a level of academic virtuosity that enables them to shine in the classics, but only Attilio Labis concentrated primarily on that genre. Cyril Atanassoff revealed a gift for character in ballets by Béjart and Petit, while both Michaël Denard and Jean Guizerix have worked in modern-dance genres as well as classical ballet.

The brilliant young Demi-caractère dancer Patrick Dupond and the more Classical Charles Jude now lead a new generation among whom Eric Vu-an already stands out. Other equally outstanding French male dancers made their careers mainly outside the Opéra: the poetic George Skibine (French-trained though Russian-born), impeccable virtuosi René Bon and Serge Golovine, and the dramatic Vladimir Skouratoff and Denys Ganio. Only the reluctance of many Frenchmen to leave France (Jean-Pierre Bonnefous with New York City Ballet being a notable exception) has prevented these dancers from being as internationally celebrated as their talents deserved.

Denmark, on the other hand, has exported many of its best male dancers in recent years. This small country inherited the Italo-French tradition from August Bournonville, a student of Vestris. He set a tradition mainly of Demi-caractère dancing that was preserved by his successor Hans Beck. However, it was when Harald Lander took over the Royal Danish Ballet in 1930 and sent it touring abroad that male dancers made the strongest impression. While the mainly Classical Børge Ralov and Henning Kronstam, the brilliant Demi-caractère dancers Fredbjørn Bjørnsson and Niels Kehlet and mimes such as Niels Bjørn Larsen based their careers in Denmark, many others found fame abroad. Poul Gnatt was a pioneer, leading the way for Erik Bruhn, the virile, technically brilliant and dramatic Flemming Flindt, Peter Schaufuss and others. Egon Madsen, a Dane who (exceptionally)

The Toreador was August Bournonville's most triumphant
role, both for the vivacity of his dancing (in Spanish
style) and the complete conviction and clarity of his mime.

did not study at the Royal Theatre, became possibly the
finest of the Stuttgart Ballet's many male stars, while the
New York City Ballet has established a steady link with
Copenhagen, strengthened further by the engagement of
former Copenhagen principal dancer Stanley Williams as
a teacher at the School of American Ballet. Among their
more recent Danish recruits are Peter Martins, a successor
to the Classical tradition of John Andersen and Erik
Bruhn; and Adam Lüders and Ib Andersen. Martins began
as a dancer but subsequently succeeded Balanchine as
director of New York City Ballet. Considering the modest
size of the Danish School, it can claim almost as high a
success rate as that of the Russians.

Another of New York City Ballet's stars, the Classically
pure Helgi Tomasson, illustrates the way an exceptional
dancer can appear suddenly from an unpromising background, for he was born and received his first training in
Iceland, a country with no great ballet tradition. Equally,
establishing a tradition does not by any means guarantee
producing stars, as the Dutch experience illustrates. In
spite of sporadic earlier efforts, dance began to be taken
seriously as an art form in Holland only after the Second
World War. Since then, two companies of international
standing have arisen, and several choreographers among
whom Hans van Manen and Rudi van Dantzig are pre-
eminent; but many of the best male dancers have come
from overseas, and only one Dutch male dancer, Jaap
Flier, has emerged who could be called great. Flier is a
versatile artist at his best in dramatic character roles – and
he was one of the pioneers of post-war Dutch dance, so
owes his achievement to nothing but inborn talent.

It may be a paucity of good teaching which inhibits the

development of great dancers in particular countries. It certainly explains why, although ballet has established itself widely in Germany over the past three or four decades, its male stars mostly come from other countries. A few have, however, begun to show the way forward. Notable among them are Peter van Dyk of the older generation, the Classical stylist Heinz Klaus in Stuttgart, Heinz Bosl in Munich (who died sadly young), another Classicist, Peter Breuer, in Düsseldorf and the intelligent Character dancer Max Midinet in Hamburg. In contrast, for all the iconoclasm of his choreography, the insistence of Maurice Béjart on first-rate classical teaching for his dancers, together with his flair for bringing out latent talent, has developed in his Brussels-based Ballet of the Twentieth Century not only notable individual talents, led by the Argentine-born Jorge Donn, but also something unique: a male corps de ballet that surpasses the women, and shows collectively a standard of dancing that elsewhere would be expected only among soloists.

Another European company with impressively high standards of male dancing throughout its ranks (although less well-known abroad for political rather than artistic reasons) is that at the Budapest Opera House. Excellent Hungarian teachers, supplemented by coaching from Russian guest teachers, ensure a grounding which is developed in a repertory drawn from both East and West, as well as from local choreographers. Viktor Fülöp, Ferenc Havas, Viktor Róna and Iván Nagy of the older post-war generation, and more recently Gyula Harangozó Junior (son of a famous choreographer), Gábor Keveházi, Ferenc Barbay and Ivan Markó, have won a wider reputation through appearances with other companies or in festivals. Other countries within the Soviet sphere of influence also produce sound dancers; Poland has a tradition of great Character dancing, with Leon Woizikovsky and Yurek Shabelevsky, both stars of the touring Ballets Russes, as outstanding examples. Sweden has produced some fine dancers, among them Jonas Kåge and Niklas Ek, based (like the Austrian Karl Musil) on a long tradition, whereas the Cuban Jorge Esquivel, the Venezuelan Yanis Pikieris and several technically assured Japanese dancers have all been developed by countries newly concentrating on ballet. In Spain, of course, dance talent is mainly channeled into the flamenco tradition which produced the eminent Vincente Escudero, Antonio, and José Udaeta.

Nowadays, Britain and, to an even greater extent, the United States, contribute far more than most countries to international ballet, even though ballet took root comparatively late in both. Britain produced a notable choreographer, John Weaver, nearly three centuries ago, and a British dancer named Simon Slingsby made a career at the Paris Opéra at the end of the eighteenth century, but on the whole, Britain used to rely mostly on foreign dancers. Anton Dolin, who was most successful in the great classical roles, was the first Englishman to become an international ballet star, followed by Frederic Franklin, who worked mainly as the Demi-caractère star of Ballet Russe de Monte Carlo in America. Robert Helpmann, who succeeded Dolin at Sadler's Wells, was basically a dramatic mime, but the British repertory, with its legacy of Maryinsky ballets, allowed him to develop a true princely style. He has been followed stylistically by Michael Somes, Donald MacLeary and David Ashmole. John Gilpin, with Festival Ballet, was a Classical artist of rare purity, as the Royal Ballet's Anthony Dowell has been since (although the latter is hard-edged compared with Gilpin's soft fluency).

Many of the best English dancers have excelled in the Demi-caractère tradition, able to assume both Classical and Character roles with conviction. Among them are Harold Turner (a lively technician of the early days of Sadler's Wells), Brian Shaw, David Blair, Christopher Gable, David Wall, Stephen Jefferies and Wayne Eagling, all of them from either Sadler's Wells or the Royal Ballet; the Scottish Ballet's Vincent Hantam is in the same league. Dancers with Ballet Rambert, notably Walter Gore, Hugh Laing and Jonathan Taylor, have tended more to the Character tradition, like the Royal Ballet's supreme comic dancer Stanley Holden. The English tradition of long narrative ballets has resulted in a rich array of actor-dancers excelling in period or costume roles, which also offer a chance for older artists to contribute, avoiding the immature effect inherent in short modern ballets in which all the performers must be (or try to look) young. For a long time, Britain drew extensively on dancers from the overseas dominions, including Alexander Grant from New Zealand and many dancers from Africa, but those countries (like Canada and Australia) have since developed their own companies, which now have first call on native talent.

For a long time, the United States too relied heavily on imported dancers, both men and women, with only occasional exceptions. One such was John Durang, famous for thirty-five years from 1784 for his hornpipes

George Balanchine (right) and Jerome Robbins as beggars
in their joint *Pulcinella* at the 1972 Stravinsky Festival.

and harlequinades; another was George Washington
Smith, who began as a clog dancer but, after dancing with
Fanny Elssler's visiting company, became in 1846 the first
American Albrecht in *Giselle*, only five years after the
ballet's Paris premiere.

In this century, visits by the companies of Genée,
Pavlova (with Mordkin) and Diaghilev whetted an appe-
tite for ballet which independent productions by Fokine
and Bolm temporarily met, but first-class ballet was not
regularly available until the arrival of Colonel de Basil's
Ballet Russe de Monte Carlo in 1933. Starting with mainly
European dancers, the company gradually recruited more
Americans, among them Leon Danielian and Nicholas
Magallanes, who (like most dancers during the pioneer-

ing years of American ballet tradition) both danced also
with other companies. When American Ballet Theatre was
founded in New York in 1940, its policy was deliberately
international. In its early days, its stars included Dolin and
the Russian-born André Eglevsky and Igor Youskevitch,
and it has continued to recruit its principals from all over
the world as well as inviting many guest stars. All the
same, some local dancers of great talent soon emerged,
notably John Kriza and Jerome Robbins; later came Scott
Douglas and Bruce Marks; and more recently Fernando
Bujones and Robert LaFosse. American Ballet Theatre
repertory required that they all be versatile, concentrating on Demi-caractère roles, although Marks proved
a noble Classical dancer and Bujones a Classical virtuoso.

The true Classical tradition in America is rooted firmly in
the School of American Ballet founded in 1934 by George
Balanchine. From this grew the American Ballet

(1935–41), where Lew Christensen and William Dollar showed themselves fine Classical dancers, and subsequently New York City Ballet. At first its male dancers were inferior to the women, although Nicolas Magallanes (Mexican by birth), Francisco Moncion (from the Dominican Republic) and local talent represented by Herbert Bliss, made a good showing, until others such as the extrovert Jacques d'Amboise, elegant Arthur Mitchell and brilliant Edward Villella pushed standards to a high level. This has been maintained not only by importing a strong contingent of excellent Danish dancers but also by the steadily rising quality of recruits from the School; Bart Cook and the brothers Daniel and Joseph Duell are already well established, and a galaxy of younger dancers are clamouring for attention. In addition, Americans who began their careers elsewhere, such as Sean Lavery, have been recruited.

Balanchine's influence is one factor that has helped push standards higher throughout the United States, where even modest local companies can expect male dancers of ability. Of the other major companies, the Joffrey Ballet has never lacked fine Demi-caractère dancers such as Christian Holder and Gary Chryst, while Eliot Feld has looked for a strong dramatic quality in his dancers. Feld's own dancing showed the influence of one of America's unique contributions to the dance: the genre of musical shows introducing first-rate dancing as an essential part of the dramatic action.

This tradition can be traced back to the extravaganzas of the nineteenth century, among which the most famous example was *The Black Crook*. At that time, dancing in such shows was primarily balletic, but musicals were given enhanced vitality by the introduction and development of other dance styles. One of these, loosely called jazz dancing, was a response to the popularity of jazz music, and has not been universally defined. Tap dancing, however, developed its own specific technique from a combination of European 'step dancing', (such as jigs and clog dances, where the feet made their own percussive music while the torso generally remained fairly rigid), with the more syncopated rhythms and looser use of the upper body and arms deriving from African dance traditions.

Naturally, it was black dancers who did much to establish tap dancing as an art in America, among them John Bubbles and Bill Robinson (known by his nickname 'Bojangles'). Although white dancers soon adopted the form, it was as a competitive sport in Harlem that its

characteristic virtuosity developed. Consequently, it began as a man's dance and, in spite of a few outstanding women practitioners (among whom Ginger Rogers outshone all rivals) it has been mainly the male tappers who have made most impression. Ray Bolger, whose career was made entirely in stage and screen musicals (including *On Your Toes* and *The Wizard of Oz*) showed its possibilities for expressing character and comedy, which were taken up by others such as Gene Kelly, Donald O'Connor and Sammy Davies. Fred Astaire found an easy elegance comparable with that of classical ballet, while Paul Draper used the form to create little cameo solos presented as a formal dance recital.

Because musicals were primarily theatrical entertainments, they drew on any kind of dance that suited their purpose: tap, jazz or social dance, ballet or modern, eventually evolving a kind of versatile free form that mingled several of these sources within one production. Gower Champion, who began his dance career by performing in night clubs with his wife Marge, was influential in that development through his work as performer and choreographer, opening the way for the more recent developments of Bob Fosse and Michael Bennett. Both turned from dancing careers to make much bigger names as choreographers and directors, giving the dance prime place in shows such as Fosse's *Dancin'* and Bennett's *A Chorus Line*.

Jazz (and hence jazz dancing) was a specifically American invention. Another art form generally associated with America is the movement known generically as modern dance, although in fact it began simultaneously, independently and spontaneously in America and Europe. In its short lifetime of less than a century, modern dance has developed more different styles than classic ballet has done in more than two hundred years. This is partly because it began as an attempt to let other arts and social movements influence the dance, and partly because it has always been led by strong-minded individualists, keen to break the mould of convention.

In the short-lived European (mainly German) expressionist school, Alexander von Swaine was one of the few men to make a big reputation primarily as a dancer, although the theories of Emile Jaques-Dalcroze and Rudolf von Laban, and the choreography of Kurt Jooss were widely influential. The first American pioneers were women, Isadora Duncan and Ruth St Denis, but the latter was soon joined by Ted Shawn, whose dramatic and

The great choreographers of modern dance were usually also the supreme interpreters of their own work.

Merce Cunningham, left, even when he lost the youthful springiness seen here in his *Totem Ancestor* (1942), remained unsurpassed for the detail, timing and authority of his dancing.

Paul Taylor's sense of comedy is manifest (right) in a solo from *The Book of Beasts*, but he was unmatched too for the range, from gentle lyrical power to overwhelming sudden impetus, in his solos.

José Limón's immense dignity, and imposing physique (below) were seen to great effect in tragic or dramatic roles by himself and his artistic collaborator Doris Humphrey.

athletic style did much to break down prejudices against men dancing; he later consolidated his solo efforts by founding an all-male group of dancers. Martha Graham's codification of a teaching method for modern dance has influenced almost all her successors, many of whom first won attention as members of her company, even though they later developed in many contrasting ways. Among them were Erick Hawkins, who devised his own gentle but strong style; Merce Cunningham who, in collaboration with avant-garde musicians and painters, pushed the boundaries of dance through many bold experiments to a new classic (though not 'Classical') style; and Paul Taylor, whose dancing embraced lyrical and wildly comic extremes. All three were outstanding dancers as well as important choreographers; another Graham dancer was the splendidly expressive Bertram Ross.

Doris Humphrey, a contemporary of Martha Graham, influenced the powerfully dramatic Mexican dancer José Limón, and in California Lester Horton developed an independent style, also vividly dramatic, from which

sprang Alvin Ailey and others. Alwin Nikolais's more abstract approach, a reaction against the emotionalism of others, produced one exceptional male dancer, Murray Louis, who then found his own inventive style, as did Louis Falco from Limón's company. After tours by Graham, Cunningham, Taylor and Ailey, a passion for modern dance began to catch on in Europe, fostered by the London Contemporary Dance School and Company directed by another of Graham's former partners, Robert Cohan. Robert North and Patrick Harding-Irmer (respectively American and Australian) are among its most notable products. During the mid-1960s, several European companies experimented with combinations of ballet and modern dance: one such was Ballet Rambert in Britain, whose young soloist Christopher Bruce blossomed into one of the best exponents of the hybrid style.

Styles of dance continue to proliferate, but classical ballet still attracts the most eager audiences, and its exponents (especially the protean Nureyev) have shown themselves able to adapt to modern idioms on occasion. In spite of all these changes, a strong and continuing tradition prevails, as can be seen in the following pages which illustrate a representative selection of the dancers who have been mentioned. They have been arranged in roughly chronological order but are divided into two groups according to whether they fall primarily into the Classical, or the Demi-caractère and Character categories. To some extent, a gifted artist may prove versatile enough to make classification difficult, almost arbitrary, and the greatest dancers entirely transcend such pigeon-holing. That is why some of these elect are discussed and displayed individually in the final chapter.

Alvin Ailey (opposite, left) tapped a vein of expressive dancing to blues, jazz and spirituals in his early solos, which he developed into the basis of his – mainly black – company's repertory.

Murray Louis (opposite, right) was the best exponent of Alwin Nikolais' unemotional dances, but for his own choreography and company he has explored a style that is often witty and whimsical.

Robert Cohan (above, in his own solo *Vestige*) was a soloist with Martha Graham and her frequent partner, but afterwards cut short his freelance dance career to become founder-director of London Contemporary Dance Theatre.

Louis Falco (right) made dances for himself and others of outstanding energy, unconventional informality and an evident pleasure in life.

Pavel Gerdt (1844–1917), seen left as Bacchus in Petipa's *The Seasons* at the age of 55, had a career as distinguished as it was long, and was acknowledged the greatest *danseur noble* of his time. Born in St Petersburg, he studied at the Maryinsky School, won praise while still a student, and graduated into the Imperial Ballet, becoming a principal dancer at 22. Ballerinas appreciated him as a superb partner but, in the practice of the time, he would only perform the pas de deux (for instance in *Don Quixote* and *La Bayadère*), while another dancer acted the role. Not until Petipa staged *La Fille du Danube* in 1880 was he given a chance to show his full abilities, acting in a famous mad scene as well as dancing.

Gerdt was already nearing 50, and plagued by knee injuries, when the most famous ballets of Petipa and Ivanov – *The Sleeping Beauty, The Nutcracker, Swan Lake* – were created with him in the leading male roles, but at the time he still looked almost boyish on stage: slim, fair-haired and handsome. His fine, intuitive acting style enabled him to continue in mimed roles: creating the villain Abdurakhman in *Raymonda*, performing some of Fokine's early ballets, and making his farewell as the comic suitor Gamache in *Don Quixote* when almost 72, less than a year before his death.

As a teacher, Gerdt helped form Pavlova, Karsavina, Fokine and many others. He jealously guarded the Classical tradition and worked by demonstration and correction, not theory. He passed to his best pupils the soft, flowing use of the arms which was one of his own gifts, together with the expressive movements and exceptional beauty of line which were achieved by complete freedom from affectation and with manly grace.

Vassili Tikhomirov (1876–1956) was only 22 when this picture was taken of him as Mars in Ivan Clustine's *Stars*, but already he was leading man of the Bolshoi Ballet and chief teacher at its school. He became the prime creator of the Classical-Heroic style of dancing that has been the Bolshoi's speciality ever since.

Born in Moscow, he trained there and was ready to graduate at 15, a year too young to join the company, so he was sent to St Petersburg where he spent two years attending Gerdt's classes and watching Johansson's class for ballerinas. He based his own teaching on theirs but developed it further by studying physiology.

Although invited to stay at the Maryinsky, Tikhomirov chose to return home. Often dancing with his pupil Yekaterina Geltzer (whom he married), he excelled in active roles – notably in *Raymonda* and *Le Corsaire*. His style was admired for its athletic plasticity and clear, vivid characterization.

He had success dancing abroad, with Geltzer in Gorsky's *A Dance Dream* (London, 1911), and partnering Anna Pavlova on her 1914 tour. But he preferred to devote himself to the Bolshoi, directing the company and school from 1925 until ill-health forced him to retire in the 1930s.

He insisted on reviving the old classics, mounting *The Sleeping Beauty* (which he remembered from its earliest seasons), *La Bayadère* and Act II of *La Sylphide*, but his new production of *Esmeralda*, starring Geltzer and himself, broke fresh ground with its dramatic and popular manner. In 1927 he was responsible, as director, joint choreographer and leading dancer, for *The Red Poppy*, the first and probably most successful example of a ballet on a socialist, patriotic theme of modern adventure – a far cry from the way his career began.

Mikhail Mordkin (1880–1944), seen above with Pavlova in a Boyar dance, was born in Moscow. He studied with Tikhomirov and soon rivalled his master's popularity thanks to a splendid physique, handsome face and virile manner. His gift for drama made him well suited to Gorsky's ballets, including a revised *Giselle* and the exotic *Salommbô*. Diaghilev was delighted to get Mordkin for the 1909 Paris season, but ambition soon drove the dancer to tour independently with Pavlova. Mordkin's bare legs and passionate manner thrilled audiences in their *Autumn Bacchanale* and his *Bow and Arrow Solo*, but when it became obvious that Pavlova was the star, Mordkin grew disgruntled and left to form his own group for a time. The Bolshoi took him back and made him ballet master, but after the Revolution he left and settled in America. Though his looks and performing career both dwindled, the Mordkin Ballet that he formed from his pupils there eventually became the nucleus of American Ballet Theatre.

Alexei Yermolayev (1910–1975) is seen left as Basilio in *Don Quixote*, a ballet he helped transform by his virtuosity (he invented many new steps for it) and his powerful, virile style. Born in St Petersburg, he was 14 when he entered the ballet school there, graduating with honours after only two years. In 1930 he was transferred as a principal to the Bolshoi in Moscow where he spent the rest of his life, becoming a teacher when he stopped dancing about 1960.

His gravity-defying debut as the God of Wind in an old Petipa ballet, *The Talisman*, was an augury of what he would achieve. The bold spaciousness of his Classical dancing enabled him to play Siegfried and Albrecht, and he was an exceptional Bluebird, but his individual gifts were best shown in ballets needing a dramatic attack: *The Flames of Paris*, or Tybalt in *Romeo and Juliet*, a fierce interpretation preserved in a film with Ulanova.

Seen above with his wife Natalia Dudinskaya in *Giselle*, **Konstantin Sergeyev** (born in 1910 in St Petersburg) was for many years the epitome of the Classical-Romantic male dancer in Russia. Although he first studied ballet only at evening classes, he danced Siegfried and Albrecht at 18 with a touring company before further study won him entry to the Kirov Ballet at 20. Before long he was creating leading roles in some of the most famous Soviet ballets, opposite Ulanova in *Lost Illusions* and *Romeo and Juliet*, and later with Dudinskaya in *The Bronze Horseman*.

As a choreographer, he tackled comedy in *Cinderella*, and also modern themes (*The Path of Thunder* was about racism in South Africa), but his main preoccupation was reviving and revising the classics. Those were the works where his traditional style and gently lyrical manner were best seen, and where he set a standard that maintained Leningrad's historic pre-eminence for the next generation to follow.

Michael Somes, seen below in his first leading role as the Young Man in Ashton's *Horoscope*, arrived at a lucky time to join what became the Royal Ballet. Born in 1917 in Gloucestershire, he first studied ballet locally, but joined both the school and the fledgeling company at 17. His youthful freshness was soon used by Ashton, for the young Somes had a lyrical quality that was rare among the few English male dancers of the time and suited the style Ashton was developing. The 24 roles that Ashton made for him over the next 30 years included most of his greatest successes, from the agony of *Dante Sonata* to the innocence of Daphnis, the pure dancing of *Symphonic Variations* to the drama of *Ondine*.

In the classics he was a sound, reliable supporter for his ballerinas, more retiring, in the old tradition, than his successors, and he achieved his widest fame during his many years as Fonteyn's nobly self-effacing partner.

André Eglevsky, nobly romantic in *Swan Lake*, below, combined the handsome physique and presence of the pure *danseur noble* with a phenomenal virtuosity: huge soaring leaps, marvellously controlled slow pirouettes, an ability to hang as if seated in the air for double cabrioles. His almost casual brilliance was manifested particularly in a pas de trois from *Paquita* that Balanchine mounted specially for him.

Born in Moscow in 1917, he grew up in France, studied with émigré teachers there and joined de Basil's company at 14. After a decade of immense youthful promise with various Ballet Russes companies (during which Fokine created roles and revised *Les Sylphides* for him), Eglevsky spent most of the 1940s dancing the classics for American Ballet Theatre and the Cuevas Ballet. He then became leading man of New York City Ballet, where he set new standards by his dancing and, after retiring in 1958, by his teaching.

George Skibine (1920–81), seen below in John Butler's melodramatic *Sebastian*, had a poetic fervour that gave conviction to such a role. It was even more appropriate for roles such as the poet in Balanchine's *Night Shadow*, or in the romantic light ballets like *Annabel Lee* or the amusing *Idylle* which he choreographed for himself and his ballerina wife, Marjorie Tallchief.

Born at Yasnaya Polianka in the Ukraine, he grew up in France (his father was in Diaghilev's corps de ballet), and had difficulty in establishing his career until, after war service, the Marquis de Cuevas saw the power of his strong stage presence. It enabled him to dance the classics, sharing roles with Eglevsky, as well as the dramatic ballets in which he excelled. Skibine's innate style and intelligence brought him for a while to the directorship of the Paris Opéra Ballet, 1958–62, and he later directed the Harkness and Dallas Ballets.

Igor Youskevitch (above), born in 1912 at Piriatin, Russia, grew up in Yugoslavia and competed in the 1932 Olympic athletics before starting his dance career. He worked during the 1930s for Nijinska, Woizikovsky and de Basil, coming to prominence with Ballet Russe de Monte Carlo as the officer in *Gaîté Parisienne* and partnering Alicia Markova in *Seventh Symphony*.

Youskevitch's innate dignity made him an ideal *danseur noble*. He joined American Ballet Theatre in 1946 and established a superb partnership with the Cuban ballerina Alicia Alonso, most memorably in *Theme and Variations* which was created for them by Balanchine as a distillation of pure Classicism.

Serge Golovine (left), a virtuoso of pure Classical style, was born in 1924, and began dancing in Monaco, the place of his birth. Taken into the Paris Opéra by Lifar, he left to become star of the Cuevas Ballet in 1950. Exceptional clarity and lightness enabled him to soar and dazzle in his solos, though a thoughtful, withdrawn nature gave his dancing depth as well as brilliance. When Nureyev joined the company, they alternated as the Prince and the Bluebird in *Sleeping Beauty*.

Besides classics ranging from *La Sylphide* to *Spectre*, Golovine had many modern roles, and a wish to experiment made him start his own group in 1962, later directing the Geneva Opera Ballet and teaching. His 1973 production for French television of *Petrushka* with Nureyev, later mounted at the Paris Opéra, is probably the best of modern times; and in 1976 he gave his farewell performance at the Opéra playing Petrushka himself.

Donald MacLeary's Albrecht (above) in *Giselle* was one of many classic roles in which he and Svetlana Beriosova formed an outstanding partnership, noted for their shared grasp of rich romantic style. Born in Glasgow in 1937, he spent his whole career with the Royal Ballet, first in the smaller company (where he and Lynn Seymour were chosen by Kenneth MacMillan to portray the adolescents in *The Burrow*), then moving to Covent Garden as a principal at 22. MacMillan made many roles for MacLeary, sometimes comic or dramatic but usually lyrical, and he played Onegin for John Cranko as guest in Stuttgart. It was in the classics,

however, including modern classics by Ashton – *Cinderella, Ondine, Sylvia* – that he excelled as a noble partner and elegant soloist. MacLeary officially retired in 1975 to become a ballet master but has danced since in emergencies or as a guest for Scottish Ballet and others.

Flemming Flindt's Don José (far right) in Roland Petit's *Carmen* is one of the dramatic roles in which his powerful sense of theatre proved memorable. However, his exceptionally strong technique – including *entrechats dix* and triple *tours en l'air* – and strict Danish schooling also made him at

home in the classics. He danced both the international repertory and his Bournonville heritage, outstanding equally as James in *La Sylphide* or the acting role of Edouard in *The Life-Guards on Amager*. Born in 1936, he was a principal in his home town of Copenhagen at 21, and joined the Paris Opéra Ballet as étoile in 1961. He also danced as guest star with the Festival, Rambert and Royal Ballet companies in Britain, Ruth Page's Chicago Opera Ballet and many others. He was director of the Royal Danish Ballet from 1966–78, and is now director in Dallas.

Nicolai **Fadeyechev**'s line in the air, as he soars gently but massively during the Prince's solo in *Swan Lake* Act III, reveals the qualities that led him to be picked for the role at the age of 20, only a year after joining the Bolshoi Ballet. Born in Moscow in 1933, he grew up to reveal the tall, upright bearing of the natural *danseur noble*. His supple elegance was able to reconcile the foppishness of the old Bolshoi production of *Swan Lake*, where Siegfried wore gloves and heeled shoes in the first scene, with the modern Soviet desire for a convincing characterization.

When the Bolshoi Ballet first travelled West in 1956, he also partnered the legendary Galina Ulanova in *Giselle* (a ballet in which he had danced for the first time only that year), and their performance is preserved in a film shot on the Covent Garden stage. Two years later he returned to London to play Albrecht in another film, with Nadia Nerina as Giselle, for BBC television.

Fadeyechev has also appeared in modern ballets, in Oleg Vinogradov's modern-dress *Asel*; as Danila, the dreaming, heroic carver in *The Stone Flower*; as the husband, with Maya Plisetskaya, in her *Anna Karenina*; and as Don José in Alberto Alonso's *Carmen Suite*. But his whole physique and personality seemed designed by nature primarily for the princely roles in the old classics. Besides being a delight to audiences, his performances in these were an example, inspiration, and an unattainable peak for many of his fellow-dancers.

Maris Liepa has the fair hair and splendid physique that seem characteristic of his native Latvia. He also manifests strong style inculcated at the ballet school in its capital, Riga, where he was born in 1936 and studied until sent to the Bolshoi School at 14. After graduating, he danced for a year back in Riga, then in 1956 joined the Moscow-based Stanislavsky Theatre Ballet as a principal. In 1960 he transferred to the Bolshoi. His sunny good looks and romantic manner made Liepa admirable in the classics, with a notably fine presence in *Chopiniana* (above) –

Les Sylphides with its original title preserved in Russia. But he also had a superb flair as a dance-actor. Plisetskaya made Vronsky for him in *Anna Karenina*, and his most celebrated role was the Roman general Crassus in *Spartacus* (right, with Nina Timofeyeva as Aegina). Arrogantly proud, lascivious, fearful in danger and unscrupulous in stealing victory, it was a performance of richly complex motives displayed with absolute clarity.

Yuri Soloviev (1940–77) graduated from the ballet school in his home town of Leningrad in 1958, at the same time as Nureyev and simultaneously with Vasiliev in Moscow. Of the three, Soloviev was the purest Classical dancer. He made his debut as the Bluebird in *The Sleeping Beauty*, a role in which the astonishing height of his jumps and the softness of his landings remain unchallenged, as does the pliancy of his line, curved triumphantly in flight (see also page 22). Later he played the Prince in that ballet, his ardent manner recorded in the 1965 Kirov film.

On the opening night of the Kirov's first London season in 1961 he danced Danila in *The Stone Flower* (left), where the heroic intensity and convincing sincerity of his acting were as impressive as his phenomenal technique. He had another role calling for tragic feeling and high heroism in *Leningrad Symphony*, an evocation of the courage and sufferings of that city's inhabitants under wartime siege. Soloviev had many other parts made for him in modern ballets, among them, surprisingly, the comic role of God in a cartoon-strip treatment of *The Creation of the World*. Above all, however, he is remembered for his brave spirit in heroic roles and the gentle generosity of his dancing in the classics, as a Siegfried of noble reticence in *Swan Lake* and an Albrecht in *Giselle* (right) whose remorse was deeply felt.

In 1977, at a time when the Kirov Ballet was deeply disturbed by dissension and arguments, Soloviev was found dead in his dacha outside Leningrad, a gun by his side. He was 36, his prodigious talent cut cruelly short.

Arthur Mitchell (left, in *Agon* with Allegra Kent) led a breakthrough for black dancers in classical ballet. Born in 1934 in New York, he studied at the School of American Ballet and danced first in modern companies and musicals, but his extraordinarily pure elegance and smooth, cat-like style ensured him a place in New York City Ballet at 22. A year later he created, with Diana Adams, the intricate, long pas de deux in Balanchine's *Agon*. His humour was seen in *Interplay* and as a guest Mercutio at Stuttgart, but he was also a complex, erotically poetic Puck, and the focal figure of Balanchine's *Requiem Canticles*, a memorial to Martin Luther King. King's death provoked Mitchell to cut his own career short in order to form the Dance Theatre of Harlem and bring it to international fame.

Helgi Tomasson's dancing (above, in *Tchaikovsky Pas de Deux*) is almost too transparently perfect for the widest acclaim, but connoisseurs rejoice in his pure style that reveals the choreography's shape with utmost clarity. Born in Reykjavik, Iceland, 1942, he studied in Copenhagen, where he danced in the Tivoli Gardens, and New York. He joined the Joffrey and Harkness Ballets, subsequently winning the silver medal in a Moscow competition when Baryshnikov won the gold. However, the turning point of his career was joining New York City Ballet in 1970. Robbins gave him roles in *Dances at a Gathering* and *Goldberg Variations*; Balanchine made solos in *Baiser de la Fée* and *Vienna Waltzes* using Tomasson's grasp of difficult phrasing; and an informed audience appreciated his virtuosity in the company's classic works.

Cyril Atanassoff (left, in *Flower Festival at Genzano*) has danced as a guest all over the world since going to Jacob's Pillow in America at 22, but his main career has been at the Paris Opéra. Born in 1941 at suburban Puteaux, he joined the company at 16, won promotion in his first year and was an étoile at 23. An innate desire to entertain marked him out even more than his powerful technique. Although dancing all the classic leads with success, his most memorable roles have therefore been those needing flamboyance, such as *Etudes*, or where he had a strong character to play. These include the victim in Béjart's *Rite of Spring*, creating the rapacious priest Frollo in Petit's *Nôtre-Dame de Paris*, or the infatuated Muffat in his *Nana*, with a tormented solo like an insect trying to get upright off its back.

Béjart's *Firebird* was made for **Michaël Denard** (above left) – its affirmation of courage ideal for his forceful technique and optimistic manner. Courage was seen in his career too: born in 1944 in Dresden, he was brought up in provincial France, only having his first ballet lessons at 16. He struggled to make a career in small local and touring companies before getting into the Paris Opéra at 21 by open competition and working his way to étoile at 26. Eagerness to dance took him as guest to many countries, including regular visits for years to American Ballet Theatre. His heroic style brought him leads in the classics (including *Giselle* at the Bolshoi), but is seen at its most personal in diverse specially-made roles ranging from Petit's Proust ballet to Merce Cunningham's modern-dance *Un Jour ou deux*.

Jean Guizerix (above right in *La Péri*) is by training, physique and technique among the purest Classical dancers of the Paris Opéra. This was acknowledged when the Kirov Ballet invited him and his ballerina wife Wilfride Piollet to dance *Swan Lake* and *Giselle* in Leningrad. But they are temperamentally drawn more to experiment and innovation. Their careers at the Opéra (which Guizerix, born in 1945 in Paris, entered aged 18, becoming étoile at 24) have run parallel; they like to work with small groups using their own choreographic efforts. Guizerix's greatest roles are those which combine his classic strength with an individually expressive quality: as Balanchine's Apollo, struggling towards godhead; in Paul Taylor's lyrically serene *Aureole*; and as the tormented, Byronic hero of Nureyev's *Manfred*.

Iván Nagy, seen above with Natalia Makarova in *Swan Lake*, achieved his greatest fame as a steadfast and self-effacing partner; Margot Fonteyn and Makarova among many others were eager to have his support because of their entire confidence that he would show them at their best. Born at Debrecen, Hungary, in 1943, he had handsome good looks and a background of training at the exceptionally fine Budapest school in his favour. This, combined with experience in the Hungarian State Ballet with its very high standard of male dancing, stood him in good stead when he moved to the United States in 1965.

Once there he first danced with the National Ballet of Washington, then in 1968 briefly with New York City Ballet before joining American Ballet Theatre. Although several choreographers made roles for him, it is as an exponent of Classical Romanticism that he has chiefly excelled, dancing in *Swan Lake*, *Giselle*, *La Sylphide* and *La Bayadère*, until an injury forced his early retirement from the stage in 1978.

Jean-Pierre Bonnefous danced Balanchine's *Cortège Hongrois* (right) with his wife, Patricia McBride. It is an adaptation of dances from the old Russian classic *Raymonda*, and thus makes a link between the European background of Bonnefous' early career and its development in New York. Born in 1943 at Bourg-en-Bresse, France, he began at the Paris Opéra, where his glamour and natural ability helped him to be promoted to étoile at 22; Béjart picked him for his own *Damnation of Faust* while Roland Petit chose him for the dazzling young hero of *Nôtre-Dame de Paris*.

He danced as a guest in Frankfurt, Berlin (where Balanchine first encountered him), Leningrad and Moscow, where he performed in classics like *Giselle* and *Swan Lake*. Invited to join New York City Ballet, he soon mastered the more involved and muscularly tense style of Balanchine's Stravinsky ballets, *Violin Concerto* and *Symphony in Three Movements*, although Balanchine used him also as Violette Verdy's partner in the deceptively slight-seeming Ravel *Sonatine*, which emphasized style, poise and musical phrasing. Latterly troubled by injuries, Bonnefous turned increasingly to choreography, but made a memorably funny Monsieur Jourdain in Balanchine's *Le Bourgeois Gentilhomme* with McBride and Nureyev.

David Wall's absolute involvement in every role, apparent from the moment he joined the Royal Ballet's touring company at 17, brought a meteoric rise. Born in London in 1946, he was a principal by the age of 20, good enough for Fonteyn to pick him as partner in *Swan Lake* and *Sleeping Beauty*, and to have a dazzling pure-dance role created for him by Ashton in *Sinfonietta*. A flair for acting through dance was the secret of his success in the classics, seen equally in tragi-comic dissolute roles such as *Knight Errant* (which Antony Tudor made specially for him) and *The Rake's Progress*. Moving to Covent Garden, Wall's range continued to be challenged, by Ashton's ballets, from *Symphonic Variations* to *Two Pigeons*, and the classics (including *La Bayadère*, right) on one hand, and MacMillan's dance-dramas on the other. He played Romeo and Mercutio alternately, and both leads in *Manon* – in which his unscrupulous Lescaut (left and above) is a notably sharp-edged, bitter creation.

Vatcheslav Gordeyev is a shining example of the *danseur noble* among the present generation of Bolshoi dancers. Born in Moscow in 1948, he studied there and graduated at 20. Handsome, virile, with apparently unbounded energy, he soon began to play the leading parts in the standard classics, beginning with Yuri Grigorovich's production of *The Nutcracker*. At 25, he won a gold medal in the Moscow ballet competition, entering with his wife Nadezhda Pavlova as his partner. They often dance together in a repertory that allows Gordeyev to show a bright technique with copybook perfection of leaps, turns and beats in *The Sleeping Beauty* (left) or *Giselle* (below). He has been featured in many of the ballets of the company's director, Grigorovich, notably as Romeo (right). When he played the title part in *Spartacus*, leading the revolt of slaves against their Roman masters, his dancing was admired for its youthful impetuosity but had less fire than others had shown in the role. It seems that it is in the more romantic side of the classical and recent repertory that Gordeyev has found his natural place.

Tall, with bold features, spectacularly blond hair and showy musculature, **Alexander Godunov** backs his striking looks with a virtuoso technique noted especially for turns and leaps. Born in 1949 in Riga, Latvia, he studied there and in Moscow, spent three years with Moiseyev's small-scale Young Ballet, then joined the Bolshoi as a soloist in 1971. His debut there was in *Les Sylphides*, but it was in dramatic rather than lyrical roles that he made the strongest impression: a Siegfried of brooding majesty and brilliant solos in *Swan Lake* (below), an electrifying Spartacus, a steely Tybalt. He shared the 1973 Moscow gold medal with Gordeyev, and became Maya Plisetskaya's regular partner after Fadeyechev. He toured France as Claudio in an undistinguished ballet based on Shakespeare's *Much Ado*, then left the Bolshoi amid great publicity during their 1979 New York season. Joining American Ballet Theatre, he danced only a limited repertory of classics including *Don Quixote* (left, with Makarova) and *La Bayadère*, and was stood off by the new director, Baryshnikov, in 1982. Despite wide tours with various ensembles before and since, in the West Godunov's talent remains enigmatic although unmistakable.

Frank Augustyn (above, as Colas in *La Fille mal gardée*) has had his career helped and hindered by the accident of his Canadian nationality. Born in 1953 in Hamilton, Ontario, he was the best male dancer to come from the National Ballet School. He joined the National Ballet at 17, becoming a principal two years later, when Nureyev, seeing his poetic aura and resilient technique, insisted on him for the Bluebird in his *Sleeping Beauty*. Since then Augustyn's long, slender but tough elegance has been displayed in many standard classic and romantic roles. But the lack of notable Canadian choreographers has held back the development of individual expressiveness; at 30, his best work could be ahead.

Jonas Kåge danced Romeo (opposite) in Nureyev's version, but MacMillan's first brought him to notice with the Royal Swedish Ballet at 19. Born in 1950 at Lidingö, he could have enjoyed an honoured career in his home land but chose to try his fortune abroad. He joined American Ballet Theatre in 1971; his powerful build and rugged good looks made Kåge a valued partner there and subsequently at Stuttgart, the Balanchine-dominated companies in Geneva and Zurich, and also London Festival Ballet. His robust stamina is ideal for Nureyev's demanding version of *The Sleeping Beauty*, *Romeo and Juliet* (he was the first Benvolio before he danced the lead) and *Manfred*.

Daniel Duell (below, in Jerome Robbins' *Sketchbook*) is among the first of a generation of native-born American men who have transformed New York City Ballet over the past decade, bringing it a general standard of male dancing that formerly existed only among its leading men. It is the result of a planned policy: Duell (born in Rochester, N.Y., in 1950 but brought up in Dayton, Ohio), and his equally gifted young brother Joseph, were both found for ballet by a nationwide scholarship programme, then developed in the School of American Ballet under Stanley Williams' teaching. The assured, poised classic style of both Duell brothers in the Balanchine and Robbins repertory is enhanced by a fresh, personal attack, each different and distinctive. It brought Daniel Duell steady advancement from his first solo, in Robbins' *The Goldberg Variations*, with a sudden leap forward when chosen by Peter Martins for the latter's first ballet, the tough, casual but intricate *Calcium Light Night*.

Ib Andersen, born in 1954 in Copenhagen, was picked by visiting choreographers, who must have perceived his nascent talents, almost as soon as he joined the Royal Danish Ballet. He appeared in Rudi van Dantzig's *Monument for a Dead Boy*, and as Romeo in John Neumeier's version. Made a principal at 20, his brilliantly precise technique and elegant line enabled him to consolidate success in the Danish and international classics and Harald Lander's *Etudes*. In 1978 Flemming Flindt recreated for him one of Bournonville's most celebrated and flamboyant roles in *The Toreador*. But Andersen's slight reserve held back his star quality until he joined New York City Ballet in 1980; there Balanchine put a bloom on his romantic presence in *Ballade* with Merrill Ashley, and made his speed and timing glitter in *Mozartiana* with Suzanne Farrell, while Robbins brought out his humour in *Piano Pieces*.

Bournonville's ballets were the heritage of **Adam Lüders** (below). Born 1950 in Copenhagen, he started his career with the Royal Danish Ballet. Beryl Grey found his tall figure right for the London Festival Ballet where he spent two years before joining New York City Ballet as a principal in 1975. Although he has continued to dance Bournonville both there and as guest in a French staging of *La Sylphide*, his unusually long limbs can look uncomfortable in those small steps. It took Balanchine's eye to discern an individual quality in Lüders and help him to develop it. He has learned to use his exceptional height commandingly in a pure Classical role such as the Tchaikovsky *Piano Concerto No 2* (*Ballet Imperial*) – which is like a distillation of *The Sleeping Beauty* into an abstract shape. In Balanchine's last major work, *Robert Schumann's Davidsbündlertänze*, Lüders' troubled, angry solos become the embodiment of the composer's spirit.

Although American born and bred, **Sean Lavery** (above) came to New York City Ballet from outside. Born in Harrisburg, Pennsylvania, in 1956, he studied locally, then in New York with Richard Thomas and Barbara Fallis. His first engagement was with the San Francisco Ballet, 1972–4; he then went to Frankfurt. There he danced Balanchine ballets and local creations, showing an inexhaustible energy and open style, added skill in partnering to his well-rounded solo technique, and became leading man in his second year. Returning home, he was accepted for New York City Ballet in 1977 and made a principal in 1978. His height and strong though slender physique make him ideal for leading classic roles, but Balanchine also made parts for him exploiting other qualities, from the sharply angular *Kammermusik No 2* to the old-world courtesy of the first section of *Vienna Waltzes* and the courtly formality of *Square Dance*.

Jean-Yves Lormeau (above, with Noëlla Pontois in *Sylvia*) is very nearly the perfect embodiment of pure Classicism. His well-proportioned, handsomely muscled physique, his noble countenance and gentle deferential smile, his fine bearing and impeccable manners are all devoted to glorifying his partner and presenting the ballet as a classic ritual. In a modern work however, such as Tetley's *Voluntaries*, that manner looks out of place: he has the strong technique one expects of an étoile at the Paris Opéra, and supple strength in the difficult adagios, but not the sense of entire dramatic involvement. Born at Dallart, South Vietnam, but based in Paris for the whole of his career, it is the classics in which he is best seen: the old French style of *Sylvia*, for instance, with choreography in direct succession from Mérante's 1876 original, or Petipa's *Sleeping Beauty* (rather than *Swan Lake*, where again modern taste demands more dramatic bite). Neumeier's *A Midsummer Night's Dream*, among modern works, makes perfect use of him as a monumentally detached, beautiful, self-sufficient Oberon.

Charles Jude's exotic features make him an obvious choice for Robbins' *Afternoon of a Faun* (right, with his wife Florence Clerc) or Nijinsky's *L'Après-midi d'un faune* but it was the extraordinary suppleness and resilient precision of his dancing that won him success from an unlikely start. Born 1953 in Mytho, South Vietnam (with a French father and Vietnamese mother), he began dancing in Nice at 15 only because the music course he wanted at the Conservatoire was full. Joining the Paris Opéra Ballet at 18, he caused a sensation three years later dancing beside Nureyev in Paul Taylor's *Aureole*. Nureyev chose Jude to understudy him in Glen Tetley's *Tristan*; Grigorovich, mounting *Ivan the Terrible* in Paris, cast Jude as the romantic Kurbski and later in the tragic title role. An étoile at 24, Jude created Romeo in Grigorovich's new version, but an accident forced him off-stage for almost two years. He returned in 1981 with new strength in the classics, where his ideally proportioned body and pure style are seen to advantage in *Swan Lake*, *Giselle*, *La Bayadère* and *Raymonda*.

Fernando Bujones has the technique, personality and style of a superstar awaiting full recognition. Born in 1955 in Miami, of Cuban parents, he began studying in Havana, then in New York at the School of American Ballet. In 1972 he joined American Ballet Theatre, winning the Varna gold medal in 1974, competing against much more experienced dancers. ABT made him a principal but Baryshnikov's arrival in the West drew attention away from Bujones, who has spent much time as guest star with many leading companies.

Slim, quick, with an unsurpassed technique, Bujones dances with rapier-like sharpness in showpiece duets such as *Le Corsaire* (opposite) and in a range of classic roles from the lively *Don Quixote* (right, above) to the romantic *Giselle.* Both qualities combine in Bournonville's *La Sylphide* where his electrifying jump and open elegant style join with the expressiveness that Tudor helped develop in dramatic parts in his *Undertow* and *Shadowplay.* Ashton's *La Fille mal gardée* (right, below) exemplifies the lyric qualities that Bujones has consciously added to his exhilaratingly joyous virtuosity.

Asaf Messerer has been a life-long leader of the Bolshoi Ballet and one of its greatest dancers. Born in 1903 in Vilna, he did not see his first ballet until he was almost 16 and only then began studying, first with Mordkin, then with Gorsky, the choreographer. Entering the Bolshoi School when it reopened after the Revolution, he joined the company in time to dance Siegfried in Gorsky's 1922 production of *Swan Lake*. Encouraged by actor friends and supported by the experimental mood of the time, Messerer's quest for realistic character made him a pioneer in cutting out all the conventional mime in favour of natural gestures. He had exceptional elevation and developed a virtuoso technique, introducing steps such as the still rare triple *tours en l'air*.

Messerer transcended categorization and continued to play *danseur noble* roles, including *The Sleeping Beauty*, while giving vent to a fiery personality and developing an interest in grotesque movement that made him shine in Demi-caractère and broad character roles equally. In *The Flames of Paris* (right) he danced Philippe, a role combining a bravura technique and impetuous acting. He was Nur-Ali, leading the Khan's warriors in wildly virile dances in the last act of *The Fountain of Bakhchisarai*, and introduced two acrobatic solos into *The Red Poppy*. With his wife, Irina Tikhomirnova, and his sister Sulamith, Messerer was sent on foreign tours during the 1920s to show the best of Soviet dancing abroad.

Although excelling in roles of such wild nature, Messerer was devoted to the Classical tradition as preserved by Tikhomirov. He taught from the start of his career, took charge of the Class of Perfection at the Bolshoi in 1942, and continued there after he stopped dancing in 1952.

Othello (right) was one of **Vakhtang Chabukiani**'s creations for the company he directs at Tbilisi, his birthplace and the capital of Georgia. Its vivid expression of fiery, deep passions is typical of his work as dancer and choreographer. Born in 1910 to a poor family, he was given classes by a local ballet teacher, then sent to Leningrad where, too old at 16 for the full-time course, he was accepted for evening classes but rapidly taken into the main school when his great talent became apparent. Graduating in 1929, he danced Siegfried before the end of his first season and was the Kirov's leading man by the end of his second. A lean, athletic body and virile, overwhelming personality joined with a forceful technique to make his a unique presence to which the young Nureyev was compared. He danced, observers said, like a whirlwind or an eagle, yet his *Swan Lake* had a polished glory. He proved the ideal hero for the new brand of Soviet ballet created in the 1930s: *The Age of Gold, The Flames of Paris, The Fountain of Bakhchisarai, Lost Illusions.* In his own ballets, notably *Laurencia*, based on an inflammatory tragedy by Lope de Vega, he continued that tendency, first at the Kirov and from 1941 in Tbilisi (though he still danced sometimes in Leningrad). Chabukiani also played a vital part in the preservation and transformation of the classics. He danced Albrecht, the Bluebird and Basilio with superb style; more significantly, he amended the choreography of many roles for greater virtuosity. The *Corsaire* pas de deux owes its present world-wide fame as a showpiece to his new choreography; so do the Diana and Acteon pas de deux (from *Esmeralda*) and large parts of *La Bayadère*. Some of his unforgettable dancing survives on film.

Stanislas Idzikowsky (1894–1977) had the most perfect technique of any man in Diaghilev's Ballets Russes, but his tiny stature kept him from romantic roles except the exotic *Spectre de la rose* and the mocking Harlequin in *Le Carnaval*. So, though he had a great success as the Bluebird, the roles most closely linked with him were those Massine made specially to show his crisp brilliance and lively nature, among them the Snob in *La Boutique fantasque* (right) and dapper Battista in *The Good-Humoured Ladies*. Born in Warsaw, Idzikowsky began his career in London, studying with Cecchetti and dancing in music halls. He ended it there too, as a teacher, with his last virtuoso role, made for him by Ashton in 1933, partnering Markova in *Les Rendezvous*.

Compared with Idzikowsky's Demi-caractère brilliance, his compatriot **Leon Woizikovsky** (1899–1975) was a robust Character dancer. Important supporting parts rather than leads were mainly created for him, but they were by Massine, Nijinska and Balanchine, and ranged from the golfer in *Le Train Bleu* (opposite, with Lydia Sokolova) to Fate in *Les Présages*. There were also fine comic roles in *Les Matelots*, *Les Biches*, *Prodigal Son* and *Concurrence*. He took over many major parts, too, inventing a thrilling new death (spinning on his head) in *Scheherazade* and rivalling Massine himself in *The Three-Cornered Hat*. Born in Warsaw, he returned there to direct a company after his proud dancing career with Diaghilev and various later versions of Ballets Russes.

David Lichine (1910–71) was a dancer of immense glamour who sprang to prominence with the beginning of de Basil's Ballet Russe in 1932, taking over the role Balanchine himself danced (on the opening night only) in their first creation, the mysteriously atmospheric *Cotillon*. His dashing manner and charm were shown also in such roles as the King of the Dandies, and later the Hussar, in *Le Beau Danube*. He excelled in comedy but could also reveal a preening voluptuousness in other ballets, such as in Massine's *Les Présages* (seen left), a role which also brought out an heroic quality in warlike struggles against Fate. His romantic ardour in Massine's symphonic ballets is shown also with Irina Baronova (below) in *Choreartium*. Born at Rostov-on-Don, Lichine was brought up in France and studied with Egorova there, dancing with Rubinstein's and Pavlova's companies before joining de Basil. From the 1940s he continued as a freelance dancer and choreographer. His own ballets included melodramas such as *Francesca da Rimini* and *Infanta*, but his dancing qualities are better exemplified by the high spirits and sunny comedy of his best and most enduring work, *Graduation Ball*.

Yurek Shabelevsky, born in 1911 in Warsaw, had the crisp technique to dance Idzikowsky's old part of the Snob in *La Boutique fantasque*, and the robust sense of character to take over Woizikovsky's comic role of the Beggar in *La Concurrence* (right). Handsome and virile, his presence in de Basil's company during the 1930s reveals not only the continuing importance of Polish male dancers in the 'Russian' ballet but also the strength and power expected from their performances. His roles in the older ballets confirmed his wide range: the sensitive Petrushka as well as the warrior chief in *Prince Igor*, and in *Le Carnaval* he danced both Eusebius and Harlequin under Fokine's supervision when he joined American Ballet Theatre for their first season. There he was also the first Colin in Nijinska's production of *La Fille mal gardée*. He continued his work subsequently with a touring company of his own and engagements in South America, Italy and New Zealand.

Though he created roles in works by Ashton, Balanchine, Massine and others, **Hugh Laing**'s supreme achievement was collaborating as dancer, and sometimes designer, in most of Antony Tudor's ballets. Born in 1911 in Barbados, Laing studied in London and Paris with Craske, Rambert and Preobrajenska. He joined Ballet Rambert in 1932, moving with Tudor to found the London Ballet in 1938, then in 1940 he became a founder-member of American Ballet Theatre where he remained until he retired in 1956, apart from a three-year spell from 1950 with New York City Ballet. His smouldering personality and overwhelmingly handsome presence (seen below with Maude Lloyd in Ashton's *Valentine's Eve*) were used also in *L'Après-midi d'un faune*, Balanchine's *Prodigal Son* and Ashton's *Illuminations*. The most unforgettable of his Tudor roles was the arrogantly strutting Young Man from the House Opposite, the incarnation of sexual desire in *Pillar of Fire* (opposite, with Nora Kaye), but they all benefited from his intelligence and understanding: the patient Waiter in *Judgment of Paris*, the impetuous Lover in *Jardin aux Lilas*, the psychopathic hero of *Undertow*. Even in *Romeo and Juliet*, the Tudor/Laing combination brought on stage a sense of real life.

Frederic Franklin is too much a gentleman, on stage and off, for his role as Stanley in *A Streetcar named Desire* (above, with Mia Slavenska) to be typical, but it indicates the range of a dancer who was acclaimed equally as Danilova's partner in the classics and in works made for them by Balanchine, and for his many great Demi-caractère roles. Born in 1914 in Liverpool, he studied there, in London and in Paris, but danced only in music halls and cabarets until the Markova-Dolin Ballet was formed in 1935. From them he went to Ballet Russe de Monte Carlo, where he became leading man and ballet master, and worked afterwards in America as director of several companies. The Champion Roper in *Rodeo* is perhaps his most individual creation: blithe, debonair, nippy and irresistible.

Gene Kelly was nearly 30 when he was first invited to Hollywood, thanks to his success in the title part of *Pal Joey* on Broadway. He had begun dancing in his mother's school at Pittsburgh, where he was born in 1912, and worked his way through law school by teaching children to dance and playing in summer stock, arriving in New York in 1939. Hollywood brought him Judy Garland as an early partner in MGM's *For Me and My Gal* (below), and they were together again in Minelli's *The Pirate*, where Kelly's acrobatic bravado was prominent. His greatest gift was for the joyous exuberance epitomized in the picture (left) from MGM's *An American in Paris*. That film's 17-minute ballet with Kelly and Leslie Caron indicated the 1950s tendency to inflated 'artistic' sequences that reached their culmination in *Invitation to the Dance*. Kelly grew tired of the adulation heaped on the title number of *Singin' in the Rain*, but the happy simplicity of that is what will be best remembered of his work, just as the location shots on the streets of New York, filmed in five days, were the highlights of his film version of *On the Town*, rather than the set ballet sequences. At his best, as an old-style hoofer with great gusto and flair, Kelly brought to the screen a lively transformation of ordinary people's fantasies into movement.

Oedipus in *Night Journey* (left) is among many roles by Martha Graham to which **Bertram Ross** brought dramatic intensity and weight of movement rarely seen since. Born in Brooklyn in 1920, he did not start dancing until almost 30, after war service and studying painting, when a psychiatrist persuaded him that defying his father's disapproval would solve his problems. He joined the Graham School and quickly became a soloist in the company. The amazingly fierce and erotic St Michael in *Seraphic Dialogue*, giving St Joan her mission; the Revivalist in *Appalachian Spring*, beguiling but frightening his followers; proud Agamemnon and apprehensive Orestes in *Clytemnestra* were among the parts on which he stamped an unrivalled expressiveness. Since 1973 he has worked on his own choreography, alone or with small groups, in search of innovation and meaning in dance.

The extrovert hero (right) of *Who Cares?* is the ideal role for **Jacques d'Amboise**, mixing the all-American boy-next-door of showbiz dreams with a modern-dress Apollo leading his muses to Gershwin music. Balanchine made the part for him, one of many since d'Amboise (born at Dedham, Mass, in 1934) joined New York City Ballet at 16 – though Ashton used him first in a leading part as Tristram in *Picnic at Tintagel*. D'Amboise projects an almost transparently uncomplicated stage personality but is able to tackle equally the original Stravinsky *Apollo*, the old-style Classicism of *Raymonda Variations*, the modernism of *Movements for Piano and Orchestra* or the romantic atmospherics of *Meditation*. He often provides a firm partner for the unpredictable Suzanne Farrell, as in the poetic *Davidsbündlertänze*, and proved suited to the cinema too in *Seven Brides for Seven Brothers*.

Alexander Grant (left, as the blustery Meath Baker in *Enigma Variations*), was born in 1925 in Wellington, New Zealand, but studied at the Sadler's Wells Ballet School. His technique could encompass a pure classic role in *Scènes de ballet* or virtuoso displays such as in the *Swan Lake* Neapolitan dance or *Homage to the Queen.* But his genius really lay in acting through dance, creating an unmatched gallery of characters. The little barber in Massine's *Mam'zelle Angot*, both touching and comic, brought him to fame, and he was a noted Petrushka, but his greatest roles were an astonishing series of Ashton creations. The most notable of these were the sad but dazzling Jester in *Cinderella*, the mysterious and powerful Tirrenio in *Ondine*, fierce Bryaxis in *Daphnis and Chloë*, the funniest, most poetic Bottom in *The Dream* (see page 22), and many others, above all the incomparably complex Alain in *La Fille mal gardée.* Although retired from dancing to take up directing (in Canada 1976–83), he has still appeared in new cameo parts.

Warlike Polynices in *Antigone* (right) was one of many vivid roles made for **David Blair** (1932–76) by John Cranko, showing his brilliant technique and flair for drama or comedy. He was the first and best Captain Belaye in Cranko's *Pineapple Poll*, marvellously nimble in the hornpipe, his strong, virile personality able to make the most of comically effete touches in the character.

Born in Halifax, Yorkshire, Blair had a tough shrewdness mixed with his showy stage personality. At Sadler's Wells and Covent Garden, his bravura and commitment shone in all the big classics of the Royal Ballet; on Michael Somes' retirement he became Fonteyn's regular partner for a time, as well as partnering Markova, Beriosova and Nerina among others. However, the Demi-caractère roles were his real domain, and for both Ashton and MacMillan he created great characters: a cocky but tender Colas in *La Fille mal gardée* and a dazzlingly flamboyant Mercutio.

Mikhail Lavrovsky's Spartacus (left) was a physical achievement of great power, even though it lacked the vehement emotions of Vasiliev in the role. Comparison with that close contemporary and fellow Bolshoi star somewhat overshadowed Lavrovsky all his career but could not eclipse a power in his movements that made him soar over the stage like a tiger pouncing. Born in Tbilisi, 1941, he was brought up to dance by his choreographer father (Leonid Lavrovsky) and ballerina mother, Elena Chikvaidze, and took the role of Romeo in his father's most famous ballet. However, it was the bolder, more heroic roles that suited him best from the start of his career with the Bolshoi in the early 1960s: Philippe in *The Flames of Paris* (his first role), or Basilio in *Don Quixote*. His closest association has been with the choreographer Yuri Grigorovich, whose wife Natalia Bessmertnova is Lavrovsky's usual partner in ballets such as *Spartacus* or *The Legend of Love*.

Valeri Panov's wild, thrilling and eccentric jumps in *Harlequinade* (right) are typical of his wholly individual style, but he was also a memorable if self-willed Petrushka. Born at Vitebsk, Byelorussia, in 1938, he studied at Vilnius, in Lithuania, before joining the Leningrad ballet school. The Kirov did not find him Classically pure enough, so he was sent to the Maly, Leningrad, as a leading dancer, achieving quick success in its more theatrical style. After losing Nureyev, and with other men injured, the Kirov acknowledged Panov's idiosyncratic virtuosity and took him on in 1963 to dance the bold heroic roles, starting with *Don Quixote*, though he gladly enlarged his range with *Hamlet*. Personal and political pressures made him apply to leave Russia, but he was released, in 1974, only after a two-year campaign, during which time his virtuosity was dimmed by deprivation. He appeared as a guest artist in many countries, but has turned increasingly to choreography, though sometimes including big dramatic roles for himself.

Paolo Bortoluzzi's faun-like pose (left) exemplifies his sensuous yet delicate style. Born in Genoa in 1938, he was first noticed at Nervi Festivals but had to leave Italy for lack of continuous opportunities there. From 1960 to 1972 he danced with Béjart's Ballet of the Twentieth Century in Brussels, touring internationally with them and creating many roles. More than anyone, Béjart understood how to reconcile Bortoluzzi's elegant precision and voluptuous, mannered style: above all in the exultation of his Bach ballet *Actus Tragicus*, as a high-aspiring Firebird, and in a solo, *Nomos Alpha*, revealing extraordinary control, balance and wit. Bortoluzzi began to accept guest engagements, especially to dance the classics, and left eventually for a freelance career including frequent seasons with American Ballet Theatre, often partnering Carla Fracci, and devising too a modern *One Man Show*.

Niels Kehlet's ebulliently springy jumps and dare-devil personality, seen below as the Joker in Cranko's *Jeu de cartes*, gave him prominence as soon as he joined the Royal Danish Ballet. So fantastically high and light were his jumps that in Copenhagen (where he was born in 1938) they joked that he must be a magic troll, not a human being. But a serious artistic quality accompanied his physical prowess. In Bournonville's classics he played not only the adventurous Gennaro in *Napoli* but romantic James in *La Sylphide*, and in modern ballets he excelled in Tetley's *Pierrot Lunaire*, Robbins' *Afternoon of a Faun* and Mercutio in Neumeier's *Romeo and Juliet*, as well as the brilliant virtuosity of *Etudes* and the bounding energy of *Moon Reindeer*. Kehlet is also one of a small group from the Royal Danish Ballet who have taken concert programmes of Bournonville ballets on many foreign tours.

By the time he was 21, **Christopher Gable** had created the leading roles in Ashton's lyric *Two Pigeons* (right, with Lynn Seymour) and MacMillan's *The Invitation*, had danced *Swan Lake*, and had become a principal of the Royal Ballet. He went on to partner Fonteyn with radiant style in *Daphnis and Chloë* (above, in his solo) and to dance successfully side by side with Nureyev in the *Laurencia* pas de six, but at 27 he stopped dancing for a career as an actor on stage, film – including Ken Russell's screen version of *The Boyfriend* – and television. Born in London in 1940, Gable was far above any other English male dancer of his generation thanks to the impetuous daring with which he performed, the absolute involvement of his acting, his fine physique and commanding presence. A dancer of great ability and even more promise when Nureyev first joined the Royal Ballet, he was quicker than anyone else to learn from the newcomer, and their trio with Seymour in *Images of Love* showed three true artists collaborating as equals. But for the minor injuries that impelled him to switch careers, he should have been the natural leader of the Royal Ballet; it is some consolation that he has lately returned to ballet as a teacher of high standards and dedication.

Christopher Bruce played *Pierrot Lunaire* (above) soon after Ballet Rambert changed from a classical to a modern company in 1966. The painfully youthful suffering he put into it, combined with his hard-edged dancing, helped to establish their success in the new guise. Born in 1945 in Leicester, he had already begun to win notice under the old regime as the Toreador Espada in *Don Quixote*. Now roles made for him by Tetley and by Norman Morrice (as a cruel spoiled brat in *Blind-Sight* and the slain leader in *That is the Show*) confirmed his gift for dramatic dance, as did Rambert's revival of *L'Après-midi d'un faune*. He turned to choreography, making tormented roles for himself based on everyday life (*Living Space*), war's cruel waste (*. . . for these who die as cattle*) and the poet Lorca (*Cruel Garden*), but directorial chores cut into his dancing, perhaps leaving his great gift only partly realized.

For romantic, tragic or comic roles, **Egon Madsen** had no superior among the male dancers of his day. Born in 1942 at Ringe, Denmark, he began his career with the touring Scandinavian Ballet, then arrived in Stuttgart in Cranko's first season there, becoming a principal after only one year. In one role after another, Cranko pushed Madsen's gifts forward; MacMillan, too, made the Messenger of Death in *Song of the Earth* for him, and others seized on his qualities later: Tetley as Pan in *Daphnis*, Neumeier as Armand in *Kamelliendame*. Cranko relished Madsen's mercurial and contradictory temperament, a serious clown working by intelligence and instinct. Madsen was the Stuttgart Ballet's first Siegfried in *Swan Lake*. In *Romeo and Juliet* he went from a reserved Paris to alternating as the wittiest, most touching Mercutio and the most ardent, moonstruck Romeo. The wild, anarchic Joker in *Jeu de cartes* (below) was made on his qualities, and in *The Taming of the Shrew* he turned the small comic role of Gremio (right), the suitor with a perpetual cold, into a major success. He was the youth overwhelmed with fearful love, the ideal foil to Fonteyn, in *Poème de l'extase*, and Don José driven downhill to despairing degradation by Marcia Haydée's Carmen; also the perfect embodiment of romantic infatuation and false ideals as Lensky in *Onegin*. He has directed the Frankfurt Ballet since 1981 and moves in 1984 to direct the Royal Swedish Ballet.

Wayne Eagling (above left, with Ashley Page in Tetley's *Dances of Albion*), was born in Montréal in 1950, but made his career with the Royal Ballet. MacMillan first set his liquid smoothness beside Dowell's in *Triad*. He excels in MacMillan's works, above all as an impassioned and impetuous Des Grieux in *Manon*. He dances all the classic leads too, but is seen at his best in parts that call for sharp authority: in *Apollo*, as Oberon in Ashton's *The Dream*, and in a created role in Van Manen's *Four Schumann Pieces*. In *The Tempest*, Nureyev used Eagling's highly individual gifts as a sad and fantastic Ariel. **Ashley Page** the leader among the Royal Ballet's younger men (born in 1956 at Rochester, Kent), as Ferdinand in *The Tempest* is rescued from shipwreck by Eagling. Page and Eagling share a strong dramatic presence, which in Page has so far been used most impressively as the angy young poet in the central role of Ashton's *Illuminations*, besides the *Albion* dances with Eagling.

Wayne Sleep (above, right, in the Hop-o-my-thumb solo that MacMillan made for him in *Sleeping Beauty*) was always odd man out with the Royal Ballet: too tiny for most standard roles, but with enormous personality and punch to his dancing. Born in 1948 in Plymouth, as a student he played the ebullient gypsy pickpocket in *Two Pigeons*, the virtuoso skater in *Les Patineurs* and an amiably dotty Dr Coppelius, but after graduating his best roles were almost wholly those which made use of his springy jump, whizzing turns and cheeky nature. They ranged from a bouncy role in *Enigma Variations* through a nimble solo in *Four Seasons* to the eager but puzzled son in *A Month in the Country*. Sleep soon began acting, choreography and impersonations that took him increasingly outside ballet; and he found a way to use his own unusual gifts in musicals and on television. With the experiment of producing his own jazzy, lively all-dance revue, *Dash*, he found a way to reach a wide new public as a star.

Patrick Dupond is a natural for Mercutio – seen here (right) in Grigorovich's version, but equally in Cranko's. His passion to make dancing emotionally rich, his vivid, flamboyantly wide-moving virtuosity and larger-than-life personality combine in that role. John Neumeier showed a quieter side of Dupond in *Vaslaw*, playing Nijinsky as a thoughtful creative artist. Born in 1959 in Paris, he joined the Ballet de l'Opéra at 15, won a Varna gold medal at 17, and began a reputation as a rebel when, being offered the *Don Quixote* pas de deux on returning, he wanted to dance it with the star, Noëlla Pontois. Himself an étoile at 21, he now dances the big classic leads (including *Sleeping Beauty* with Pontois) and has danced marvellously in Paul Taylor's lyrical *Aureole*. But his great gift is for creating thrilling characters in dance: as the fantastic bounding Alain in Heinz Spoerli's *Fille mal gardée*, or the hilarious Puck and officious Philostrate in Neumeier's *Dream*.

Roll of Honour

In any art one or two exceptional individuals will, through sheer quality, transcend all efforts at grouping. They are unique and unclassifiable, exerting their influence through inspiration rather than imitation. The dancers illustrated here are examples of this phenomenon and are drawn from three stages in the history of dance – the Past, the recent years of Yesterday, and the Present. Those whose reputation has survived for generations are sure of their fame; yesterday's choice can be guaranteed as having at least left a distinctive mark on their own age; today's celebrities are rather different, since they are at varying stages in their careers and can be acclaimed less confidently. But all of them have attained that international recognition which separates the true star from the local celebrity. They are all candidates for immortality.

It is tempting to draw conclusions even from this short list. Six of them, it will be noticed, are Russian; three are Danish; two are British; three American; two French; Italy, Spain, Australia and the Argentine have one each.

General standards seem to be reflected in individual excellence, but even these outstanding artists could be grouped according to their natural aptitudes; an inherent genre can be detected behind all their wide-ranging achievements. In most cases, however, they have so far transcended their original category as to render such labelling meaningless. There are two exceptions; Fred Astaire and Jorge Donn are both confined to a narrow range of dancing outside the general tradition and it is impossible to guess how they would have fared in choreography not especially created for them. But both have rightly earned a world reputation and a place in this roll of honour.

These are names which have filled theatres in many continents, set pulses racing and planted the seeds of emulation in the young. In their turn they will be able to look with pride at the youngsters who arise in the future – not to replace them, for they are by definition irreplaceable – but to succeed them.

GAETANO VESTRIS

The special merit of Gaetano Vestris, as one of his contemporaries remembered it, was 'grace, elegance and delicacy. All his steps had a purity, a finish, of which one can have no idea nowadays'.

He was born in Florence in 1728, one of seven children of Tomasso Vestris. At least three of the children made a reputation as dancers. Gaetano's elder sister, Teresa (1726–1808) studied in Naples and had already danced in Palermo, Vienna (where she briefly became the mistress of Prince Esterhazy), Dresden and Florence, before arriving in Paris, aged twenty. Gaetano and a younger brother, Angiolo (1730–1809) both followed her there, having previously danced in various Italian theatres. In Paris, they studied with Louis Dupré, who was then approaching the end of his long career as leading dancer at the Opéra.

Dupré had been admired for his graceful style and his splendid physique. Gaetano Vestris was small in build but that seems not to have detracted from his success as a pure Classical dancer. He was handsome, and vain with it: when a lady accidentally trod on his foot, and apologised, expressing the hope that she had not hurt him, his reply is reported to have been, 'Hurt *me*, madam? You have only put all Paris into mourning for a fortnight.' He was quarrelsome, too, and had to leave Paris for a time after an argument with the ballet master, Lany (Teresa Vestris's lover), whom he threatened with a sword.

For a time, Gaetano Vestris held the post of choreographer, but seems not to have had much success in that sphere, and soon relinquished it. His gifts were for dancing, and it was said that he 'gave more freedom to the "positions" already known, and created new ones'. Except for the interruption in 1754–5 following his quarrel with Lany, during which time he danced in Turin and Berlin, Vestris was *premier danseur* at the Paris Opéra from 1752 at the age of twenty-three until retiring from the stage in 1782. During the latter part of his career, however, although he continued to dance, he concentrated on directing the school and overseeing the career of his son Auguste.

As well as his virtuosity and elegance, Gaetano Vestris must have been a dancer of great expressiveness. He was influenced by the ideas of the choreographer and theoretician, Jean-Georges Noverre, who in turn had been inspired by the English actor Garrick. Gaetano's brother, Angiolo, was one of Noverre's leading dancers, and Gaetano went to dance with Noverre's company in Stuttgart. He later secured the post of choreographer for

Gaetano Vestris

Noverre at the Paris Opéra when he himself gave it up.

One of Noverre's beliefs was that ballet should get rid of the masks that were customarily worn by dancers until his day, and Gaetano Vestris is credited with being the first dancer to appear without one, in the ballet *Medea and Jason* (1770). His belief in his own good looks was possibly a contributory factor in his decision, but it was reported that he astonished the public by the dramatic force of his acting without a mask, and thus paved the way for others to follow his example.

Besides his great artistry, Gaetano Vestris never neglected the value of publicity. He claimed that 'there are only three great men in Europe – the King of Prussia [Frederick the Great], Monsieur Voltaire and me'. He appropriated the title of 'God of the Dance', formerly applied to his teacher Dupré, by having another of his brothers, Jean-Baptiste, shout it out during one of his performances. Yet this conceited and ill-educated man was undoubtedly a superb artist to have won Noverre's admiration, and for his dancing to have been described as 'a masterpiece of nobility and grace'.

AUGUSTE VESTRIS

The Parisian public called him Vestr'Allard, presumably to show their awareness that Auguste Vestris (originally named Jean-Marie Augustin Vestris) was the child of Gaetano Vestris and his former pupil, now partner, Marie Allard. But Auguste appears to have inherited more than a name from each parent; in him, the grace and precision of his father mingled with the vivacity of his mother, who was able to delight audiences with the verve and gaiety of her comedy roles (most notably in a ballet called *Sylvie*), and to move them to tears as Noverre's Medea.

Auguste Vestris was taught to dance by his father, and made his debut at the Opéra when only twelve, dancing a chaconne in a divertissement, *La Cinquantaine*. His extraordinary gifts were remarked straight away, and the next year he had another success as Amor in a ballet by his father, *Endymion*. He was appointed a soloist at the Opéra in 1776, *premier danseur* in 1778 and recognized as the leading male dancer there with the title *premier sujet de la danse* two years later, when he was still only twenty. He made his London debut the following year, appearing with his father; so great was the desire to see them that Parliament is said to have suspended its sitting. He returned to work in London for four years from 1789, fleeing from the possible consequences of the French Revolution, and danced at the King's Theatre under Noverre. In 1793 he returned triumphantly to Paris, and although he soon had a rival for fame in the person of Louis Duport (twenty or more years younger, and possessed of unusual lightness and dazzling pirouettes), he was able to hold his own. Auguste Vestris continued to dance regularly until 1816, when he was fifty-six, and nineteen years later he appeared again, dancing a minuet with Marie Taglioni.

Auguste was as conceited and difficult as his father, but his sometimes ill-mannered behaviour was tolerated for the sake of his talent. He was short and knock-kneed, but developed what was considered almost miraculous virtuosity in jumps, beats and pirouettes. Where Gaetano Vestris had been described as 'Apollo come to earth to give lessons in grace', Noverre called Auguste 'the new Proteus of the dance' – less noble, but more varied in his range. His prodigious skill in pirouettes led to a description of him in verse as the man

> '...who on one leg could do
> What erst no mortal could achieve on two.'

Gaetano explained his son's greater success with the comment that of course the boy had one advantage – himself for a father. That typical boast is at least partly justified, but overlooks the influence of his mother in endowing Auguste with greater adaptability, so that he succeeded as much in comic roles as in those of noble qualities. In this, Auguste Vestris can be seen as the predecessor of today's dancers who take on a wide range of styles.

He was also directly responsible for handing on an artistic pedigree. Just as Gaetano Vestris studied with Dupré, extended what he had learned into a greater degree of skill, and passed that on to his son, so Auguste in turn extended the virtuosity further and handed on the succession to his own gifted pupils, who included Charles Didelot and Jules Perrot, both of whom enjoyed great international success and, among other achievements, helped plant the seeds of Classical ballet in Russia. Another of Auguste Vestris's pupils was August Bournonville. The style of male virtuosity in his ballets probably gives a better idea of how the great Vestris danced than any other evidence readily available today, for the role of the ballet master in *Conservatoire* can be seen as a portrait in dance of the old master.

Auguste Vestris looks elegant in his portrait (right) but this caricature reveals the exuberance of his pirouettes.

ΤΩΝ ΜΕΝΤΟΙ ΧΗΝΩΝ ΟΥΚ
ΕΣΤΙΝ ΟΣΤΙΣ ΟΥ

VASLAV NIJINSKY

Between the retirement of Auguste Vestris in 1816 and the debut of Vaslav Nijinsky in 1907 the male dancer retreated into the shadows – an incredible eclipse of nearly a hundred years. The invention of the 'point shoe' had given women a technical advantage which fitted the new Romantic image of the ideal heroine. Men still controlled ballet from behind the scenes and they were admired as partners; some of them, such as Arthur Saint-Léon, or Carlotta Grisi's husband Jules Perrot, were undoubtedly fine dancers. But men were expected to play a secondary role – solid, manly, reliable, handsome – the ideal of a Victorian husband.

In a single evening in 1909, when Diaghilev presented Nijinsky at the première of his Ballets Russes, this whole image was overthrown by a small, fey dancer who was unimaginable as anybody's husband and virtually irrelevant as a partner. Androgynous, ambiguous, mysteriously elusive and inhuman yet charged with some unearthly passion, he switched the male ideal from the superhuman to the supernatural. The change was total, the shock profound and lasting. Vaslav Nijinsky regained supremacy for the male dancer but indelibly stamped with his own image.

In some ways this was unfortunate, for he was far from being representative of his colleagues, either then or later. To start with, he was notably unmasculine – a fact which has cast a rosy cloud over the whole concept of the male role in ballet. He was not moulded by nature to be a Hero, a Warrior or even a Lover; erotic rather than romantic, neither his dreamy Albrecht in *Giselle* ('a young faun from some Slav Arcadia') nor his haunted Siegfried in *Swan Lake* (an interpretation which might win praise today) seem to have proved very satisfying. Instead he invented – with the inspired collaboration of the young choreographer Fokine – an entirely new type of dancer. It was a total and highly personal revolution (though we can see now that it coincided with the Symbolist and Art Nouveau movements); only Nijinsky could have achieved it, only Fokine could have revealed it and only Diaghilev could have persuaded the public to accept it.

Nijinsky's triumphant but tragic career, perfectly fitting the romantic idea of the doomed genius, has become one of the best-known chapters in dance history. He was born in Kiev, the son of two Polish dancers; his sister Bronislava was to become a famous choreographer, but his elder brother Stanislav was committed to an asylum while still in his teens. Vaslav entered the Maryinsky (today the Kirov) School in St Petersburg at the age of ten, graduated into the company at eighteen and joined Diaghilev's Ballets Russes two years later.

Promoted by Diaghilev, who adored him, he quickly became the star of the company, soon taking over from Fokine as its principal choreographer as well, creating the highly original *L'Après-midi d'un faune*, *Le Sacre du Printemps* and *Jeux*. Then, during a voyage to South America he succumbed to the importunities of a rich Hungarian dancer named Romola de Pulszky, and married her.

Nijinsky (opposite) in *L'Après-midi d'un faune*, the first ballet he created and the only one to survive, based on mythical antiquity but giving choreography a new spirit.

Fokine made *Scheherazade* (the Golden Slave, top left) and *Spectre de la Rose* (above, with Karsavina) for Nijinsky, who also transformed Harlequin in *Le Carnaval* (right).

Consumed by jealousy, Diaghilev fired him by telegram; whereupon Nijinsky tried, not too successfully, to start up a company of his own. The 1914 War overtook him while in Budapest with his wife, and he was interned; with Diaghilev's help he escaped to dance in one more season with the Ballets Russes, but he was beginning to show signs of mental instability. Thereafter, he lived with his wife in seclusion until his death in 1950.

Insignificant and almost inarticulate off-stage, his tragic fate added to his legend. The mystery surrounding his personality spread even to his origins. To many people, he seemed to have literally dropped from the skies as a pure and unsullied spirit of the dance, only to be corrupted by Diaghilev who has been accused of contributing to his insanity through his sophisticated embraces. His sister's memoirs now reveal a different picture. He was already an experienced performer when he entered the St Petersburg school, a circus kid who had been entertaining the public since the age of six. His father Thomas, a successful performer on the music-hall stage, took a continuing (and critical) interest in Vaslav even after deserting the family, which was left hard up but not actually poor. While still a student Vaslav took the fancy of a rich prince who showered him with presents and set up the family in an expensive apartment. When Diaghilev appeared on the scene with his tempting offer of stardom in the West, the prince had to leave and Vaslav, now a thorough dandy, began to lose touch with his mother and sister. It must have seemed that he had sold out to success.

On the contrary, however; Nijinsky became totally committed to his art, until his foolish marriage, followed by the outbreak of the Great War, deprived him of openings for his passionate drive for perfection. That a

popular child performer should end by sacrificing his reason for artistic ideals is even more mysterious than the accepted myth of the 'holy fool'.

It is evident that he never even approximated to the ideals of a Classical dancer. Short and sturdy, with a figure whose very shortcomings he contrived to turn into facets of beauty, and a manner more beguiling than commanding, his innate type could be classified as Demi-caractère. He was not much interested in elegant 'line', technical correctness nor bravura proficiency, though he clearly had exceptional facility, including a sensational jump – quick, high and floating. His obsession was with the development of the entire body as an expressive instrument; for hours he would practice the supple use of fingers and arms rather than the basic ballet leg positions. Through instinct or intelligence, he devised a style which gave prominence to his long, strong neck, his sleek head and full, soft arms. He disguised his narrow shoulders, thick waist and short legs (he was 5 ft 4 in tall) by sinuous twists and turns, and by standing on, or even jumping onto, half-raised feet.

He made this suave and sculptured style into an instrument of feeling which has never been surpassed, radically changing the male image in dance in much the same way as Rudolph Valentino was to do in the cinema. He was an amazing actor, gifted with the ability to change his features from role to role and a constantly alert and lively expression which Vestris would have admired. He opened up whole new areas for male dancing, though his strongly mannered style limited his own range; he might have fared less well with the crisp, tart choreography which became fashionable in the twenties. But insanity plucked him off the stage at the very moment when his manner and beliefs were going out of style.

In some ways he was a lucky artist, with time, place, fashion and gifted collaborators to help him. But his extraordinary qualities, which both changed and enriched the possibilities of his successors would surely have made their mark in any circumstances. Not a trace of these survive on film; but he was exceptionally sensitive to the camera and there are many still photographs. These glimpses reveal something of the weird and original charisma in which the divine authority of the traditional hero was replaced by a pagan magic more disturbing and theatrically compelling. He was an artist to whom the label of 'genius' is strictly applicable – unique, instinctive and beyond classification.

Nijinsky's *Jeux* (left) was ahead of its time in dealing with contemporary behaviour and in dressing its three characters in a stylized version of the dress of the day, such as they might wear for a real game. Curiously, people seem to have accepted this easily, even though it was entirely different from the exotic roles in which he had hitherto appeared; what caused more concern was that the ball bouncing across the stage seemed the wrong size for tennis. Actually the games that Nijinsky and his two partners (Tamara Karsavina and Ludmilla Schollar) were playing were more to do with their relations off the court than on it. The four ballets that Nijinsky created, from *Faune* through *Jeux* and *Sacre du Printemps* to *Til Eulenspiegel*, were all remarkably different from each other and from other ballets of the time.

Petrushka (right) was, of all the roles made for Nijinsky by other choreographers, the one that has most captured the imagination of the general public as well as ballet enthusiasts. Attempts to identify the dancer with the role, seeing him as the puppet of the Old Showman Diaghilev, are clearly misplaced when seen in the light of his own achievements as a creative artist, both as choreographer and in the understanding he brought to the interpretation of the parts invented for him by Fokine and others, even to the extent that the shape of his body, neck and head seems to change from one role to another as he embodies the particular character.

LÉONIDE MASSINE

Two of the most convincing proofs of Diaghilev's flair for talent spotting were his choice of Stravinsky as composer after hearing only one orchestral piece, and his selection of Léonide Massine after seeing him, aged nineteen, in two tiny roles with the Bolshoi Ballet in Moscow. Although almost exactly Nijinsky's opposite, for many years Massine took his place as leader of the Ballets Russes (and in Diaghilev's affections too), before going on to a long international career as performer and choreographer.

Born into a large family of Bolshoi Theatre musicians, he entered the ballet school, where he stood out more for his looks (dark and slim, with coal-black hair and brown eyes – he was nicknamed 'the Gypsy' where Nijinsky had been 'Little Jap') and dramatic talent than for technical prowess. As with Nijinsky, it was clear he would not be a classical hero, but his vitality, intelligence and feeling for the stage were exceptional. He played small 'grotesque' roles as a child (a dwarf, a monkey) and enjoyed acting more than dancing, which he thought a 'mediocre form of light entertainment'. But he eventually achieved the roles in which Diaghilev first saw him: as the mysterious Knight of the Moon in *Don Quixote*, and the Tarantella dancer, needing speed, dexterity and charm, in *Swan Lake*.

Diaghilev needed a replacement for the recently dismissed Nijinsky in Fokine's forthcoming *Legend of Joseph*. Massine made little effect in the (simplified) choreography, but with his doe-like eyes and skimpy costume, he made a touching contrast to the mature charms of his temptress, and his popular success earned him a regular place with the company. He took over several of Nijinsky's parts (the erotic Faune, the bounding Golden Slave in *Scheherazade*, the jerking puppet Petrushka), besides other more romantic parts, including the poetic Eusebius in *Le Carnaval*.

Lessons with Cecchetti, the great Italian teacher, could not overcome the limitations of his technique; his muscles were hard, his manner sharply accented rather than broad and creamy; he would never have excelled in the serpentine style favoured by Fokine, but Diaghilev was surfeited with Art Nouveau fluidity; Massine's dry, wry personality and his dance style, influenced by Cubism and the movies, exactly marked this change in taste. Massine, off-stage and on, was quick, wiry, masculine, even aggressive

where Nijinsky had been softly mysterious, melting and silent; calculating where Nijinsky had been instinctive, he provided the perfect link between the hard-edged emphatic rhythms of Russian folk art with the new acerbic Parisian style – outstandingly in *Parade* (1917); he added a further piquant ingredient in the doll-like antics of the Commedia dell'arte after a trip to Italy with Diaghilev.

He was a keen, quick learner, better able than Nijinsky to hold his own among the new 'court circle' of Picasso, Cocteau and their clever Parisian friends, and Diaghilev soon entrusted him with composing a new ballet, *The Midnight Sun* (1915). The creative as opposed to the interpretive activity proved more absorbing to his essentially positive character; he was to develop it steadily and fruitfully – he composed over a hundred ballets – and as time went on it tended to overshadow his dancing achievements. He became an influential and popular figure both in Europe and America, the most admired choreographer of the thirties, and was to prove himself a bold innovator as well. Paradoxically it was to be this inspired mime and actor manqué who launched a

Massine as the Miller (left) in his own *The Three-Cornered Hat.*

Right, his first Diaghilev role, in *The Legend of Joseph.*

In one of the most famous roles he made for himself (left), Massine dances the Can-can as one of the dolls who come to life in *La Boutique fantasque* – an old-fashioned story enlivened by the vivacity of the dances. His own performance was based on tales of a real Can-can dancer, Valentine, said to look completely boneless.

Massine turned his sense of theatre to different ends in *Parade* (right), where his own performance as a Chinese conjurer was just one element in a ballet conceived by Jean Cocteau as a deliberately shocking display of modernism, with Picasso's Cubist designs and a score by Satie incorporating a typewriter among its instruments.

Massine (below) as choreographer-collaborator: posed with the designer, Matisse, and their 'mechanical' bird before the première of *The Song of the Nightingale*.

widespread controversy about 'abstract ballet' through his symphonic dance-translations.

These later activities have tended to overshadow his achievements as a dancer; yet nobody who saw him on stage can ever forget the electric charge of his personality nor the dynamic vitality and agility of his dancing. He was a master of perfectly timed grotesque movement and of a tension which gave the impression that every nerve and muscle in his body was pulled up like a spring. As an adult his legs were too awkwardly built to allow him to dance roles that involved wearing tights but his slim supple body with its tight waist and strong arms surmounted by dark theatrical features could fit the roles of the romantic poet – in *Carnaval* or *Symphonie Fantastique*, or the gallant lover – in *Le Beau Danube*, as aptly as those of the Chaplin-esque clowns he portrayed so inimitably.

He was always most at home in the parts he invented for himself – the witty, proud and passionate Miller in *Le Tricorne*, the white-faced, boneless Can-Can Dancer in *La Boutique fantasque*, the sly Chinese Conjurer in *Parade*. Perhaps his most striking quality was the ease with which he could, like Chaplin, switch instantly from comedy to sentiment and back. To that skill he added an authority which enabled him, in a scene such as the last moments of *The Firebird*, to command the stage like a Tsar. Grotesque or picturesque character acting was there transformed into an echo of true Classicism.

FRED ASTAIRE

In this cavalcade of special talent, Fred Astaire is the odd man out. He called himself an outlaw, but that label suggests defiance, which was notably lacking from his career. By coasting along the road on which he was set as a child, never deviating at the call of experiment or ambition, he raised a popular style of dance entertainment to such a pitch of perfection that it became the expression – indeed the symbol – of a whole new dance culture.

Unconsciously he marked the break in dance – also evident in the other arts – between the European tradition of the Renaissance and the demotic conventions of the twentieth century. He also pinpoints the move of dance interest from Europe to America. His approach was modern and popular, rooted in American history and social values and in an American approach to the arts. It is as close to a folk art as the Polonaise in *The Sleeping Beauty*.

The change he brought about was effected slowly, effortlessly and one might say invisibly – if that word can be applied to an artist who worked in the full glare of public acclaim. It was achieved through sheer persistent quality. Eventually the dance world woke up to the fact that an alternative dance style had been developed which could rival the old values, which depended for its origin partly on Astaire's musical gifts. From the music hall versions of American negro jazz display numbers and from European (mainly British) ballroom dancing conventions, he took and adapted whatever best suited the subject in hand. George Gershwin, Jerome Kern and Irving Berlin thought of him as not only a great dancer but 'also a great singer . . . He knew the value of a song and his heart was in it before his feet took over.'

He was born Frederick Austerlitz, in Omaha; son of a local girl and an Austrian father, a brewer who arrived in America from Vienna only three years before Frederick's birth, and soon changed his surname. Fred began dancing as the partner of his elder sister Adele, and they made their professional debut in vaudeville when she was seven, he five. (It is curious to think that he had begun his career while Nijinsky was still a student in St Petersburg.) After years touring the United States, the Astaires broke into Broadway musicals in 1917, while he was still a teenager, and soon became stars of the New York and London stage. Although often thought of as a film-dancer with a style and technique closely linked to the crafts of the cinema, Fred Astaire did not leave the stage until Adele – the more popular of the two, and the best partner he ever

had – married and retired. His long association with her coloured his whole approach to dance. They were the artistic heirs of Vernon and Irene Castle, whose elegance and skill had carried ballroom dancing into a theatrical form; Fred and Adele Astaire continued the convention of a salon flirtation as the only permissible relationship, and Fred's self-deprecating, throw-away style developed as he worked in Adele's shadow.

Deeply professional, sharply intelligent but far from reflective or visionary (his main interest off-stage was race-horses), he fell eagerly on the opportunities offered by the newly invented sound films and patiently explored the field of dance-photography. Although he was already thirty-four when he first entered a Hollywood studio, he made thirty-one of the finest dance films ever shot, sharpening his own performances to a peak of personal style. Devising almost all his own choreography, he

Astaire with his sister Adele on stage in *Funny Face* (below), and (opposite) with Ginger Rogers in RKO's film *Swing Time*.

Astaire in a characteristic sequence from MGM's *Three Little Words* (above), and (opposite) in his 'Putting on the Ritz' solo in Paramount's *Blue Skies*.

clearly relied on what he did best and most easily: a marvellously fluent, fast, twinkling kind of movement linked with great musicality to decorative taps and swinging romantic curves and pauses, with much use of plastic épaulement and wide arms (unusual in jazz dancing), and always in lively contact with his partner.

His gallantry towards his partner did not so much reflect a prince escorting his royal bride, as a young man-about-town taking a girlfriend out for the evening – witty, attentive, non-committal. He wore the accepted clothes

of a modern man (even if often heightened into the comparatively exotic form of full evening dress). His carefree style looked natural (the result, in fact, of painstaking rehearsal – although he seems never to have done a practice class in his life) and appeared, with his elfin personality, an ideal version of everyday behaviour.

Unlike Gene Kelly, he rarely ventured into ballet movement, and his range was restricted; passion, eroticism, earthy humour, grandeur or savagery were outside his scope. Like a pianist playing with the right hand only, he drew his music from the light end of the scale – the sentimental, touching, charming, unashamedly prettified world of musical comedy. His real achievement was the distillation of that well-worn art form into something pure and stimulating. Balanchine called him 'the most interesting, inventive and elegant dancer of our time'. Like an angel dancing on the point of a needle, Astaire at his best produced the frisson of a fragile feat perfectly executed.

Although Anton Dolin began his career with Diaghilev's Ballets Russes, and his seasons there helped establish him as the first British male dancer with an international reputation, he was not temperamentally much in sympathy with the Russian company or its director, and his fame rests more on what he achieved for himself afterwards. He did much to lay the foundations for what would later become the Royal Ballet and for American Ballet Theatre, but his independent nature flourished in his own ventures, which added enormously to English audiences' knowledge and love for ballet. It is above all, however, for maintaining and handing down the pure classical tradition that he will be remembered.

He was born (as Patrick Healey-Kay) the son of a horse-loving English father and an Irish mother. She had theatrical ambitions for him and sent him, aged ten, to a good dancing school near their southern English home. Soon he began working as a child actor in musical comedies, plays and even films. Seeing Seraphine Astafieva, a former Maryinsky dancer, at the Coliseum set his mind firmly on dancing, and, at thirteen, he entered her London school. From her studio, the boy dancer was engaged by Diaghilev (under the stage name of Patrikéeff) for the corps de ballet of the 1921 production of *The Sleeping Princess*, but it was not until the end of 1923, when he had already danced solos in Astafieva's presentations and taken his new stage name of Dolin, that Diaghilev offered him a contract as a soloist. He made his debut as Fokine's Daphnis, but quickly progressed to his first created role, in a work made specially for him by Jean Cocteau in 1924, a Riviera divertissement called *Le Train bleu*. Nijinska's choreography made masterly use of Dolin's charm, athletic figure, ebullient spirits and gymnastic agility, and he became a star overnight.

Diaghilev was delighted: 'He dances in a really adorable way ... Perhaps the impression is due only to the novelty of his appearance, but he does possess true style'. Dolin vied with Lifar as the favourite of the moment, but he was less assiduous, and 'got bored being taken to museums', preferring to spend time on the beach. A strong technique soon won him virtuoso roles, the 'Bluebird' duet and *Le Spectre de la Rose*, but within two years he left to dance in shows, forming (with Vera Nemchinova) his first small company, for which he choreographed Gershwin's *Rhapsody in Blue* among other things. Dolin briefly returned to the Ballets Russes for what was to be Diaghilev's last

season, dancing – among other new works – in *Le Bal* (1929) by Balanchine (who admired him in it).

At the time of Diaghilev's death in 1929, there was no established company in either Britain or America. The commercial theatre was the only refuge for most dancers, and Dolin soon found his feet in music hall and revues, making his first visit to America in one of them. He also staged the dances for Max Reinhardt's mammoth *Tales of Hoffmann* in Berlin. Back in London in 1930 he had a big success in a creation by Frederick Ashton, *Pomona*, for the opening performance of the Camargo Society (a ballet production club formed to fill the gap left by Diaghilev) and took part in many of their later performances, including a memorable *Giselle* with Olga Spessivtseva in 1932. Their productions, and the programmes by Ninette de

Right, in *Le Train bleu*, supported by Leon Woizikovsky.

Below, dancing on pointe as L'Elégant in *Les Facheux*.

For all his exceptional showmanship as a solo performer, Dolin was also renowned as a great partner, and of the many ballerinas he danced with (including Tamara Karsavina and Olga Spessivtseva, Tamara Toumanova and Carla Fracci), his name was most often linked with Alicia Markova's. *The Nightingale and the Rose* (left) was made for one of the tours in which they took ballet to audiences all over America, Britain and many other countries.

The Nutcracker (right) was a popular classic which, for many years, Dolin and Markova made specially their own, and it formed the rock on which the artistic and commercial success of Festival Ballet was founded by them in 1950. This pas de deux in particular showed their fine-spun artistry and pure Classical style at a peak of elegance.

Valois' small company in which Dolin also performed, were among the first steps towards a British national ballet. Though neither highbrow nor self-sacrificing, Dolin played a crucial role in establishing today's Royal Ballet. His genuine love of performance made him seek wide audiences and he appealed strongly to popular taste. He did not stay long, but his fame drew knowledgeable audiences who had seen him with Diaghilev; he scored the company's first big success as Satan in *Job* in 1931, and he brought to the classics authority, experience and his own ultra-traditional classical style; and by the time he left in 1935, the Sadler's Wells Ballet was firmly on its feet.

From 1935 to 1938 he and Alicia Markova led a touring company – the Markova-Dolin Ballet – with Nijinska as its ballet mistress; and most of his subsequent career was spent with similar ventures. However, he spent seven years with American Ballet Theatre, where he created the comic lead in Fokine's last ballet, *Bluebeard* (1941),

spent periods in the two rival Ballet Russe companies, and appeared – briefly – as a postwar guest at Covent Garden. London Festival Ballet was probably the most famous of the companies he helped to found; he was its leading man and director from 1950 until 1961. The last twenty years of his life he devoted his lively energies to producing, to occasional mimed roles, and to acting.

During Dolin's long career, the bright-eyed zest that probably first attracted Diaghilev persisted, while his instinctive exhibitionist panache actually increased until it verged on flamboyance. Yet the athletic natural vigour that first won him attention in gymnastic demi-caractère roles matured into a well-studied mastery of the classics and of their twentieth-century echoes such as *Les Sylphides* and *Le Spectre de la Rose*; and the generous nature that helped explain his wide popularity in those works also led him to pass on his knowledge to a long series of pupils and discoveries, whose careers he furthered as eagerly as he once did his own.

Serge Lifar

iaghilev's four male stars arrived in the company by very different routes. Nijinsky, already a celebrity in St Petersburg, virtually picked himself. Massine was chosen personally by Diaghilev; Dolin arrived with a special recommendation from his teacher. Serge Lifar, however, turned up almost by chance, but his meteoric career is a classic example of opportunity seized by the forelock.

Born a civil servant's son in Kiev, at the age of fifteen he joined the free, public classes given by Nijinska (then ballet mistress there) on the spur of the moment. A few months later, Nijinska left to rejoin Diaghilev; Lifar continued with her successor. When she eventually cabled for five of her best pupils to join Diaghilev, Lifar, now eighteen, got himself included in the party replacing one who could not be traced. Although unimpressed, Diaghilev accepted them all into the corps de ballet.

By his own account, Lifar's rapid rise from the corps was due equally to talent, hard work and seduction. Slim, swarthy and dark-eyed – a combination always to Diaghilev's taste – he did not hesitate to bring his elegant figure shyly to notice. 'At nineteen years of age,' he wrote later, 'I would have had to be devoid of intuition and sensitivity not to sense the kind of power possessed, the charm exercised.' Later, when Lifar had his nose flattened, accentuating his Asian appearance, Cyril Connolly found him 'beautiful as a rare monkey'.

Diaghilev, duly charmed, in spite of distraction in the form of Anton Dolin, set about improving his new discovery's technique by sending him for special classes with Cecchetti, but Lifar worked enormously hard to justify this. In spite of Nijinska's disapproval (she left in protest), Lifar was quickly given leading parts in ballets by Massine: *Zéphyre et Flore*, where he excelled Dolin, and, in 1925, a comic part in *Les Matelots*. He also established a great classic partnership with Spessivtseva, first in Act II of *Swan Lake*. (Later, after he had been coached by Pierre Vladimiroff, the former Petersburg danseur noble, Lifar was to dance *Giselle* with her at the Paris Opéra.)

Hard work and talent had put Lifar in a position to take advantage of his chance, fully justifying Diaghilev's sharp-eyed choice. However, the company was less strong than it had been; Diaghilev was indulging largely in self-conscious modernism: Lifar danced wearing chic factory overalls in the 'workers' ballet' *Le Pas de Acier*, and in a rigid celluloid costume for *La Chatte*. Balanchine did create two great roles for him: as the 'wild, half-human

Above, Lifar in the finest of the roles created for him with the Diaghilev Ballet, Apollo in Balanchine's ballet.

Opposite, in *The Creatures of Prometheus*, to Beethoven's music, Lifar's first creation at the Paris Opéra.

youth who acquires nobility through art' in *Apollo* (1928) and the fiercely dramatic *Prodigal Son* (1929), where the finale allowed Lifar to introduce some old-fashioned Russian histrionics.

After Diaghilev's death in 1929, Lifar was invited by Balanchine (who had fallen ill) to take over the production of Beethoven's *Creatures of Prometheus* for the Paris Opéra. Lifar did so to such effect that (after working in one of Cochran's revues in London), he became director and star of the Ballet de l'Opéra for more than twenty-five years, interrupted briefly in the forties after complaints that he had collaborated with the Germans during the occupation (his defence was of having safeguarded the dancers, including some Jews). Lifar introduced valuable reforms at the Opéra: regular ballet nights, lowering the house lights during the performances, banning the habitués from backstage privileges. He made the ballet more respected, and tried bold experiments such as a ballet performed only to percussion. Lifar was a theatrical, self-centred personality whose svelte, supple body and striking features made him an eye-catching figure with a feline charm and electric vitality. But the exotic, glamorous side of his personality, which Diaghilev had kept

Above, in his own ballet *La Nuit*, created for The Cochran Revue, 1930, which he danced with Nikitina and Balanchine. Opposite, as the young man in Balanchine's *La Chatte*, with Olga Spessivtseva in the title part.

under control, his ultra-romantic approach and exaggerated manner made Lifar less admired on his rare excursions outside the Opéra, in spite of his wonderfully plastic way of moving; and although his many ballets long dominated the Paris repertory, most disappeared once he left, and only one, the mannered but spectacular neoclassic *Suite en Blanc* (also known as *Noir et Blanc*) ever achieved much popularity outside France.

Lifar's was a self-centred artistry (he admitted that his sole gratification came from admiration by others); he courted idolization – and often deserved it. He was also an eloquent and conspicuous champion of ballet in public and in print. A supreme embodiment of theatrical glamour, he developed his own distorted kind of classicism that coloured the French approach to ballet for several decades, but he may also, by his eccentric gifts in youth, have helped spark the purer new-style classicism that Balanchine developed in America.

Robert Helpmann

The son of a well-to-do Australian sheep farmer, Robert Helpmann's early career as a child actor and dancer was encouraged by his mother, herself a frustrated actress. He had already toured extensively in revue by the time Anna Pavlova arrived in Australia when he was fourteen years old; seeing her company in Melbourne inspired him to concentrate initially on classical ballet. He joined her professional classes led by her ex-Bolshoi ballet master, Laurent Novikoff, and toured with the company; but its departure meant that he returned temporarily to plays and revues.

Below, left, in the title role of his own most successful ballet, *Hamlet*, set to Tchaikovsky's fantasy overture and showing the hero's dying dream of his own life.

Below, right, as Mr O'Reilly, manager of the Pantheon Theatre, drunkenly celebrating its destruction by fire which solves all his problems in Ninette de Valois' *The Prospect Before Us*, a comic treatment of true history.

Opposite, with Margot Fonteyn as the mysterious Woman in Ball-dress who serves as both torment and inspiration to the Poet played by Helpmann in Ashton's romantic ballet, *Apparitions*.

Encouraged by the English actress Margaret Rawlings to stage a little ballet as curtain-raiser for her touring show, he travelled to London in 1933 and auditioned for Ninette de Valois, whose small Vic-Wells Ballet was helping to fill the gap left by Diaghilev's death.

De Valois was impressed by both his achievements and his looks – slight, lively and large-eyed, with strikingly dramatic features. She thought he resembled a young Massine or Chaplin. She engaged him on the spot for the corps de ballet (a humble offer which, he wrote, made 'his whole being vibrate' with fury), but within a year he had leading roles.

The first was replacing Dolin as Satan in de Valois' *Job*, where the histrionic style of the role, with its eye-rolling echoes of William Blake's drawings, gave him a rich opportunity. He became male star of the company, replacing Dolin as Markova's partner for the classics, showing uninhibited romanticism as Albrecht in *Giselle* and Siegfried in *Swan Lake*, and later beginning a long, fruitful partnership with a fledgling ballerina, Margot Fonteyn, who learnt much from his strongly theatrical approach to ballet.

Helpmann was never more than a modest technician, but relied on personality, projection and drama. Two centuries earlier, those gifts would have fitted him to be a great dancer in the noble or heroic style. With a growing emphasis on virtuosity, Ninette de Valois' company outgrew Helpmann's contributions in that respect, but not before he had set an example of how to command the stage for others to follow.

He started choreography in the 1940s during Frederick Ashton's absence in the RAF: the intensely dramatic *Hamlet* (1942) and *Miracle in the Gorbals* (1944) fitted the dark wartime mood with their expressionist violence, besides illustrating his personal predilections in the richly introspective roles he created for himself.

Helpmann had always pursued a varied career. He took periods of leave to appear in revues and plays (mostly by Shakespeare), directed operas and plays, performed in films – not only with dancing roles as in *The Tales of Hoffmann* and *The Red Shoes*, but also with straight acting parts, as in Olivier's *Henry V*. His ballet career lasted well into his forties, and he did not give up dancing

regularly until he had helped to launch the Royal Ballet (then Sadler's Wells) in America, partnering Fonteyn in the historic opening night of *The Sleeping Beauty* in New York, on 9 October 1949.

Within this dramatic style, he had great success in ballets by de Valois and Ashton; the former's *Haunted Ballroom* and the latter's *Apparitions* both showed Helpmann as an elegant, exotically doom-laden figure. As the feverishly intense hero proceeding from foppishness to insanity in *The Rake's Progress* – a role on which he was to leave an indelible imprint – or the senile, pathetic Red King in *Checkmate* (both by de Valois) he showed his serious side, but he was at his most inspired in comic parts, including the irresistibly bibulous Mr O'Reilly in de Valois' *The Prospect Before Us* – a memorable interpretation that saved a complex and otherwise dull work. Helpmann was also responsible for discovering hitherto unrealized opportunities for clowning as the old toymaker Dr Coppelius in *Coppelia*. Sir Frederick Ashton called upon Helpmann's wit and cynical charm when creating the role of the Bridegroom in *A Wedding Bouquet* (based on a play by Gertrude Stein), and later still brought him into the more broadly comic travesty role of the bitchy Ugly Sister in his *Cinderella*.

It was chiefly for his comic characterizations that Helpmann was occasionally invited to return as guest artist after retirement, but his multifarious activities (including a long spell as director of the Australian Ballet and even making a pop record) also took in staging classic revivals (*Swan Lake* and *The Sleeping Beauty*) and demonstrating publicly (in a show produced by Maina Gielgud) the principles and practice underlying the great classic duets. He was knighted in 1968 for his contribution to British ballet.

Helpmann was a supreme example of the advantages of the Demi-caractère genre. Too slight in build for heroic Classical roles, he nevertheless contrived to make a convincing Prince through sheer artistry and musicality, as well as being a sympathetic partner. His line was always elegant and harmonious, his style lofty. But his real strength lay in sinister and comic roles: his range stretched from romantics to buffoonery, from pathos to sophisticated clowning, and he revelled in grotesque elderly roles like 'Don Quixote'. As a classicist he conveyed a kind of vulnerable poetry, as a dramatic Character dancer he has seldom been equalled and probably never surpassed.

Helpmann emphasized the diabolical aspects of Satan in de Valois' *Job* (opposite) rather than portraying him, as Dolin had, as a fallen angel.

ANTONIO

Antonio Ruiz Soler was born in Seville in 1922, and, having made his professional debut aged six in a double act with his ten-year-old cousin Rosario, boasted later that he had supported his family from the time he was eight. At first, Rosario and Antonio toured together all over the world, but his personality and skill always eclipsed hers, and when they eventually split up in 1953, he formed his own company with other partners.

His overwhelming effect on audiences as a showman (a master of such tricks as 'accidentally' losing his hat – at the same moment each night), his insistence on the highest standards of presentation in respect of costumes and lighting, his flair for arranging the raw material of Spanish dance into suites with a well-planned structure and climax: all these played a part in his success. So too did his zeal in introducing a great variety of styles into his programmes. He was probably the first dancer, for instance, to form a complete suite of Galician dances for theatrical use, with the violent vigour of the men's dances set against the wistfulness of the women.

Yet it was primarily his extraordinary rhythmic sense and gift for using dance to express a lively personality that made him an international dance star. Spanish dancing has an elaborate set of techniques (though less developed than classical ballet) and a jealously preserved style. Antonio excelled in both technique and style, but it was the impact of the man himself that drove audiences wild, distinguishing him from many other fine Spanish dancers. After a period in which Spanish dance had been dominated by women (La Argentina, La Argentinita, Pilar Lopez), he was able to restore male supremacy in that form of dance, just as had already happened in ballet.

Of the many styles he undertook with success, two stood out in his programmes. One was the zapateado, a flamenco dance exclusive to men, marked by staccato footwork and rhythmic stamping. The critic Richard Buckle, one of Antonio's most enthusiastic admirers, pointed out how, in contrast to most rivals, who stamped throughout as hard as they could, Antonio's heel-taps 'surge to a furious crescendo, then fade away to nothing, and there is a lull, as in the finale of a Beethoven symphony, before the ultimate storm breaks loose; then he climbs to a summit of crashing chords, and as we expect the last trump his great dance comes suddenly to an end, not in a thunder of footfalls, but with a delicate, supercilious snap of finger and thumb.'

In the zapateado, tradition required Antonio to disguise his tiny stature by drawing himself up as tall as possible (his slim figure helped); but he was also uniquely adept at introducing wit and humour into his dancing, sometimes making the most of his small, boyish appearance by assuming a mock pathos. His humour found its fullest scope in the bulerias that customarily ended his programmes: little solos with an element of improvisation, in which the whole company would join, guitarists and singers taking their turn among the dancers. Antonio's own contributions were swiftly sketched portraits – almost caricatures – of types and individuals, cowardly or boastful, proud or sly. During the latter part of his career, he attempted to use the techniques of Spanish dance in dramatic forms modelled on classical ballet, but perhaps his greatest contribution to the dance of his native land was the example he gave in bringing to the traditional forms a lively expressiveness as vivid as that of the ballet. That, and the way his own range extended over categories as varied as the equivalents of the neat, spry virtuoso and the character artist of classical ballet, ensure Antonio a place among the geniuses of twentieth-century dance.

Antonio (opposite) in one of the spectacular virtuoso solos which were usually the highlight of the flamenco dances he devised for himself and his company. An electrically mercurial personality and a fine concentration marked all his performances, whether classical, comic or dramatic.

Jean Babilée

There is a curious restlessness about Jean Babilée that has prevented him from remaining long with any one company and has caused interruptions to his dancing career, sometimes of a whole decade, during which he acted in films or plays, directed shows, taught or choreographed. Yet he has a charisma that burned itself into the memory of anyone who ever saw him, making him easily the most outstanding dancer of his generation.

He was born in Paris, the son of a doctor who also painted, and studied dancing at the Opéra, but he appeared there only briefly in the corps de ballet and later for one season as an invited star. His solo debut was made in Cannes, dancing the classics as a teenager; he then fought with the Resistance before making his name at twenty-two with Les Ballets des Champs-Elysées, directed by Roland Petit (himself a notable romantic dancer as well as choreographer). There, Babilée was to dance three of his greatest roles. As Bluebird, he impressed even a perfectionist critic like Cyril Beaumont, who wrote that his elevation and *brisés* (swift skimming beaten steps) 'really do suggest that he is borne by invisible wings and, like Vestris, only comes to the ground so as not to humiliate his fellow-artists'.

Yet that was almost his only success in the classics. Although his virtuosity was dazzling (and apparently effortless), his interest lay in creating characters on the stage. In Petit's *Le Rendezvous*, for instance, he played a hunchback, a role with no dancing, yet he dominated the stage. His art was most rewarding when that sense of character combined with his bravura technique, as in his two great created roles of that time. Janine Charrat made the Joker in her *Jeu de Cartes* (1945) for him; almost throughout the ballet he was leaping and twisting in the air, yet what impressed most was the sardonic authority he gave the character. Equally, in Petit's *Le jeune homme et la mort* (1946), Babilée's powerfully muscled acrobatics served to portray a passionately torn young man of the day, an existentialist (the 'in' philosophy of the time) starving in a garret, hopelessly in love, and waiting for Death to lead him away over the rooftops of Paris. When he crossed the stage in a series of three incredibly slow backward rolls, what the audience saw was less the virtuoso stunt (impressive as that was) than the pain of the young man tortured by the woman he loved.

Of his own ballets, the most memorable were probably the capricious *Til Eulenspiegel* (1949), and a marvellous illustration of classical purity and control, *Haï-kaï* (1969), using Webern's music – exact opposites in style and mood. After he had run his own company for a time, Babilée gave up regular appearances, but returned from time to time for creations that always made a strong impact: *Maratona di Danza* in Berlin, about the dance-hall marathon competitions of the twenties; a modern version of *The Prodigal Son* for Lazzini's Marseilles company; an acting-dancing role as the Devil (appearing in multiple disguises) in Stravinsky's *The Soldier's Tale*. In this production in 1971, his daughter Isabelle (child of his former wife, Nathalie Philippart, who had shared his success in *Jeune Homme* as the unloving mistress who turns into Death) played the Princess.

At the age of fifty-six, Babilée was suddenly offered another dancing comeback by Maurice Béjart, who created a solo for him called *Life*, which was premiered in New York and enjoyed a rapturous success there with audience and critics who generally dislike Béjart's creations. At sixty, Babilée was again dancing that role in Paris, still able to hold an audience spellbound through a body held under superb control and a mind that gave meaning to every movement.

Opposite and below, Babilée in the most famous role created for him – the young man driven to suicide for love in *Le Jeune homme et la mort*, conceived by Jean Cocteau and staged by Roland Petit.

Overleaf, left, Babilée rehearsing with Yvette Chauviré for a gala in Paris in 1954.
Overleaf, right, as Oedipus in *La Rencontre*, with Leslie Caron as the Sphynx on the platform above.

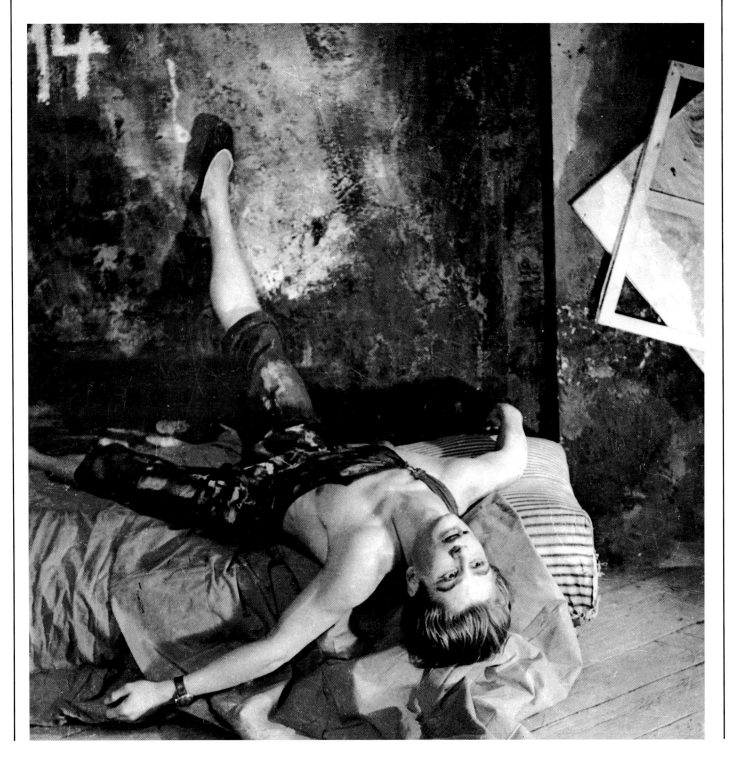

ERIK BRUHN

Erik Bruhn dominated the ballet world of his period like a rock: granite-hard, smooth, dizzily high, inscrutable, unscaleable. He carved for himself a unique path of fame, a popular hero in his native Copenhagen (where his every performance sold out at once); an acclaimed star in New York; elsewhere, a connoisseur's dancer, admired by colleagues and the informed public, but dancing always with a reserve, a cool quest for perfection that refused to 'sell itself' to an audience.

His father (an intelligent engineer whom he much later got to know and like) left the family when the boy was five, and his capable, domineering mother brought him up in an otherwise female household. He grew silent and withdrawn; dancing classes were advised as a cure. There he found his feet immediately. His well-proportioned body, unusual facial beauty and a natural musicality soon attracted attention, and at the age of nine he was admitted to the Royal Danish Ballet School. His technical progress was dazzling, yet his teachers found him introspective and inhibited; his exceptional facility seemed only to increase his detachment. Through his whole career he seemed to set up obstacles of his own devising and remained dissatisfied with his achievements.

Although his light, neat dancing, elegant carriage and clean technique ideally fitted the Bournonville repertory of the Royal Danish Ballet, Bruhn seized the first possible opportunity of gaining experience elsewhere, with the small, newly-formed Metropolitan Ballet in England. It was a wise move, for on returning to Copenhagen, he showed new qualities in productions by Massine (notably *Le Beau Danube*) and danced his first big romantic lead, as James in *La Sylphide*: his performance, a personal interpretation which brought out all Bruhn's light-weight romanticism and buoyant charm, was condemned in Denmark for departing from precedent, a view that only changed after he had been admired overseas.

Still dissatisfied, he received and accepted, in 1949, an invitation from the wealthy president of American Ballet Theatre to join the company. Not knowing that the initiative had been personal, taken without consultation with the artistic director, Lucia Chase, Bruhn was surprised by his initially cool reception. He was able to overcome it, however, to become one of the company's stars, and for the next twelve years shared his time between New York and Copenhagen. American Ballet Theatre offered him chiefly the classic repertory in which he triumphed, from his first *Giselle* in 1955, which he took on at very short notice, partnering Alicia Markova.

A turning point in Bruhn's career came with the arrival in the west in 1961 of Rudolf Nureyev. Although he had only seen a film of Bruhn made when Ballet Theatre toured Russia, Nureyev was already a great admirer of the older dancer and had said to a colleague, who criticized Bruhn's dancing as cold, 'Yes, so cold that it burns you.' Nureyev quickly sought out Bruhn and they became close friends who helped each other greatly in spite of being almost opposites in physique, style and temperament. Nureyev gained speed and precision from working with Bruhn; the latter found new energy and inspiration for his work, also perhaps a broadening of his approach.

After they had performed together in a specially devised programme in Paris, both dancers were invited to appear as guests with the Royal Ballet in London. Bruhn's *Sleeping Beauty* (it was the first time he had danced that ballet) was enormously admired, but he did not feel happy with the production. The effect of Nureyev's Kirov style proved unsettling to the Danish dancer, who – though generally regarded as the paradigm of classical excellence – declared himself 'not a classical dancer at all'. Public comment comparing and contrasting the two stars upset Bruhn; so did the Royal Ballet's decision to take Nureyev but not him as a semi-permanent guest. Soon afterwards John Cranko, in Stuttgart, created for Bruhn what he thought the finest of his remarkably few specially-made roles, in *Daphnis and Chloë* (1962), securing a performance that made the most of Bruhn's technical facility; but a fear that he could never repeat it caused a crisis that forced Bruhn to report himself unwell and depart at once.

From now on Bruhn was more of an itinerant guest star. He gave performances in Paris (with Yvette Chauviré), Copenhagen, and Milan – where he started a partnership with Carla Fracci which was to become celebrated in America; he spent a second spell with New York City Ballet (but as before there was a clash of temperament between him and Balanchine), he sustained a part-time relationship with the National Ballet of Canada and spent periods directing companies in Stockholm and Rome.

His international reputation stems from this later stage of his career – especially as he broke away at last from his classical repertoire and took on, with great success, strong character roles. His violently passionate Don José

Bruhn in his solo from the *Don Quixote* pas de deux.

in Roland Petit's *Carmen* and the magnetically charming, unexpectedly smooth and sardonic interpretation he gave to the caddish manservant in *Miss Julie* revealed a dramatic intensity which had hitherto remained hidden.

Unfortunately Bruhn's temperamental problems increased, causing him to develop mysterious pains that were only after many years correctly diagnosed and treated as an ulcer. Intermittent ill-health darkened the later years of his active career until, unable to bear the pain further, Bruhn abruptly withdrew from performing at the beginning of 1972, aged only forty-three. After treatment, he resumed work as a teacher, producer, choreographer

Below, another example of Bruhn's poise and dash in classical solos: this one from the *Nutcracker* pas de deux.

Above, as James in *La Sylphide*, dancing in the bounding, open style of Bournonville's choreography.

Right, also from *La Sylphide*, with Carla Fracci as the Sylph in an extract from the second act which they danced at a gala with American Ballet Theatre.

and director, but confined his stage appearances to the less physically demanding roles, including Dr Coppelius and the witch, Madge, in *La Sylphide*.

With his chiselled features and aristocratic bearing – princely rather than regal, for he never had the physique to suggest imperial power – he seems to have devoted himself to an ever sharper and smoother image of a kind of marble classicism. Temperamentally he was withdrawn and introspective; this aloofness gave a mystery to his performance but created a barrier which he penetrated only in his uncharacteristic character roles. His range was limited, but his record is one of unparalleled distinction.

Erik Bruhn as Jean the butler in *Miss Julie*, a dramatic role that he made so much his own that audiences in New York and Copenhagen were drawn to see him rather than the ballerina playing what is titularly the main role.

Edward Villella

Edward Villella has outstripped any other male dancer of his generation in the expression of sheer energy, overwhelming and exciting. He was unmatchable in certain virtuoso roles, especially those created by Balanchine, such as the *Tarantella* designed specifically to display the dazzling speed and high spirits of Villella and Patricia McBride, or the Tchaikovsky *Pas de Deux*, which Villella took over and transformed into a breathtaking display of exuberant leaps.

Born in New York, he began dancing because his mother wanted to keep an eye on him during his sister's ballet lessons. Although he was given a scholarship to the School of American Ballet, his training was interrupted, at his father's insistence, for four years from the age of fifteen to study at the Maritime College. Only after graduating could he go back to dancing – the profession which, by then, he wanted to pursue. He joined New York City Ballet

Villella in Robbins' *Watermill*, in which, though cast as a mainly passive observer, he dominated the action.

in 1957 and gained rapid promotion. He spent his whole career with the company, until back problems forced him gradually to withdraw from dancing in the late 1970s, but he also undertook many guest engagements which allowed him to dance a wider range of roles including *Le Spectre de la Rose* and Albrecht in *Giselle*, and to appear in Broadway musicals.

By physique and temperament, Villella's was a pure demi-caractère style, displayed to perfection in ballets such as *Harlequinade*, or the section called 'Rubies', danced to Stravinsky's *Capriccio*, in the three-part production known as *Jewels*, also created for him by Balanchine. These were roles where a brilliant classical technique was displayed with humour, wit and stamina. Besides his high spirits, however, Villella developed qualities of pride and control which enabled him to take on roles that would usually go to a man of the pure Classical type. Peter Martins, joining New York City Ballet from a Danish background, described himself as baffled and awed by Villella: 'He was a magnificent athlete, a

fantastic animal, but with an American elegance and refinement . . . I saw him fly through the air, turn blindingly fast, increase and decrease speed with unbelievable facility. I saw an intensity and electricity that threw everything before it, and made new rules for itself.'

The first leading part that Balanchine created for Villella was Oberon in *A Midsummer Night's Dream* (1962), where his conception of the story needed a short man but one capable of huge, light jumps. Villella was cast for *Apollo*, too, as well as the more obvious choice of *The Prodigal Son*, where his tremendously forceful attack made the most of the young man's eagerness to leave home, and where Balanchine's advice to think of Russian icons gave him the understanding for the quieter, more tragic moments. Pushing him in quite another direction, Balanchine used Villella as the bridegroom in his Japanese-inspired ballet *Bugaku* (1963), in which he was required to move slowly and with an impression of solemn weight.

The other choreographer who developed and enlarged Villella's gifts was Jerome Robbins. Villella's first role on joining New York City Ballet was in Robbins' *Afternoon of a Faun*; the choreographer told him that the initial idea for that ballet had come from seeing Villella, while still a student, stretching in a shaft of sunlight while he leant lazily against the barre in class. Similarly, Robbins' great Chopin ballet, *Dances at a Gathering* (1969), began as a pas de deux for Villella and Patricia McBride before he started adding other dancers and more music. Having already set Villella dances in this ballet that used (in Villella's words) 'exactly what I'm mostly about – jumping, flying around, bravura', Robbins decided to make the serene and contemplative opening solo for him too. This led to their collaboration in *Watermill* (1972), a slow, extended ballet, influenced by Japanese Noh plays, in which a man looks back on his life from the winter of age.

Apart from the brilliance of his performances, heightened by his confident manner, dark good looks and cheeky grin, Villella was an important exemplar of the emerging American style of male dancing. In his role as one of the principals in Balanchine's neo-classical *Agon*, he successfully brought the sense of a tough, self-reliant streetwise New Yorker to the ballet stage, typifying the sharp, linear, challenging approach of American ballet, with his distinct edge and attack.

Left, in Balanchine's *Prodigal Son*; right, in *Swan Lake*.

139

Rudolf Nureyev

Rudolf Nureyev is probably the most widely known dancer in history. Through television, films and a phenomenal schedule of appearances in five continents over some twenty years he has had an audience of tens of millions. That he has survived such exposure is evidence both of his character and of his quality as an artist. He manages to carry the past into the present, blending the mysterious aura of the traditional idol with the glamour of a contemporary pop-star.

The mixture of history and modernity is reflected in a career which could hardly have been more theatrical. He was born in 1938 to a family of Tartar blood and brought up in wartime poverty in central Russia. There was no theatrical tradition in the family, but from childhood he was obsessed with dancing. After some early lessons in the local opera house at Ufa, he made his way to Leningrad and applied to enter the famous ballet school. He was already seventeen – far older than the normal admission age – with only basic training, but his exceptional gifts were obvious and he was accepted. Within only three years he passed right through the course and emerged as a prizewinner at the all-Russia student competition in Moscow.

He entered the Kirov company at once, partnering its top ballerina Natalia Dudinskaya and appearing in leading roles in most of the classics. But, already, he was an outsider, and he never fitted into the tightly-knit organization of the company. After a series of rows he was finally threatened with summary recall to Moscow at the end of a season with the company in Paris, during which he had scored a huge success. Breaking away from his companions at the airport, he sought asylum in France. Independent and tempestuous by temperament, he had fought his way to the top in Russia through his own efforts; now, at twenty-three, he was entering the even tougher world of ballet outside Russia with only his talent in his pocket.

The publicity which followed his arrival in the West propelled him into the headlines like a rocket. But he himself regards the story and all that led up to it, as supremely unimportant, irrelevant to the only thing which matters to him – his dancing. His commitment to dancing is total, and he is filled with an extraordinary drive to express himself through it. It takes priority over everything and everybody.

Drive and flexibility are perhaps his greatest assets, but they form only part of his armoury. He is theatrical to the backbone, and he has particularly studied the art of reconciling dramatic gesture with classical ballet conventions. He believes that the dance style sets the tone for the acting – he has remarked that even the 'mad' scene in *Giselle* is a kind of dance variation – and he has evolved for the classics a broad approach, with a minimum of realistic 'business', to establish the character and the mood. When it comes to a dramatic climax, few can vie with him for intensity and abandon. 'Every step must be sprayed with your blood,' he says.

This impression of daemonic energy marked his style from the start. The natural 'voice' of Russian dancers is pitched lower than that of their counterparts in the West, and Nureyev – though his range is wide – is constitutionally the equivalent of a baritone, not a tenor. As the old Tchaikovsky classics were written for Russian 'voices', he has the advantage which most of his compatriots enjoy in them, as compared with the lighter, more lyrical dancer typical of the West. He has an instinctive sense of line, adjusting an arm or the angle of his head subconsciously to maintain the flow of movement from end to end of his body, but he is not built for delicate long-limbed elegance. He is (as Nijinsky clearly was) a sculptural

Opposite, at class in Rosella Hightower's studio, Cannes. Below, during a rehearsal for his British debut.

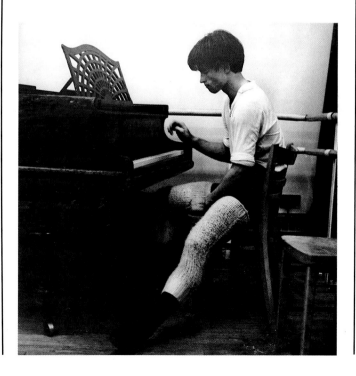

141

Above, Nureyev on stage in Paris, May 1961, rehearsing as Prince Désiré in *The Sleeping Beauty* for the opening of the Kirov Ballet's first season in the West. Then and ever since, this role has been a supreme example of his grasp of the pure Classicism handed down from Petipa's St Petersburg to the Leningrad School of his time.

Right, in the pas de deux from *Flower Festival at Genzano* on American television in 1962. This was Nureyev's first experience of the Bournonville style of Classicism, drawn from the old French school, and the occasion of his first appearance in the United States when he learned the role to replace the injured Erik Bruhn.

With Margot Fonteyn, right, in *Marguerite and Armand*, the first ballet created to use Nureyev's talents, and Frederick Ashton's tribute to the romantic quality and passionate drama of the greatest dance partnership of their time.

Below, in *Giselle*, again with Margot Fonteyn in the Royal Ballet's production (Monica Mason, right, as Queen of the Wilis): another example of the special quality of the partnership that spurred Fonteyn to surpass her past achievements in a new blossoming of her gifts.

Left, in comic mood; this mocking imitation of a butterfly's wings was one of the individual touches that Nureyev brought to the role of Franz in *Coppélia*, which he played only in Bruhn's production for the National Ballet of Canada.

A moment of tragic drama, below, in his own production of *Romeo and Juliet*, which he created with London Festival Ballet in 1977, forcing the familiar Prokofiev score to fit his own close reading of Shakespeare and of the historical and literary background of the period.

rather than a linear dancer, exploiting the contrast between his narrow, flexible waist and his powerful shoulders and back. He is very aware of the spaces enclosed by his limbs and by the interaction between himself and his partner. His arm movements are always full and generous and his legs mark out the stage patterns with emphasis. When he moves fast it is with the speed of a projectile, not a dart. He never loses the quality which sculptors call 'mass' – a kind of concentrated volume and density which lends presence to a movement.

This characteristic emerges clearly in the big leaps which were the most obvious striking feature of his first appearance. He does not shoot up quickly and lightly from the ground as though gravity did not exist; he does not skim or fly, drift or flicker. When he jumps there is a perceptible build-up of power, a tremendous thrust, and then a great lift-off: once in the air he soars and sails rather than floats. Karsavina described his leap as 'space-devouring'.

He has an instinctive panache – he is a master at swirling a cloak or flourishing a hat – and the capacity to dance

Opposite, in *Moments*, created for him by Murray Louis.

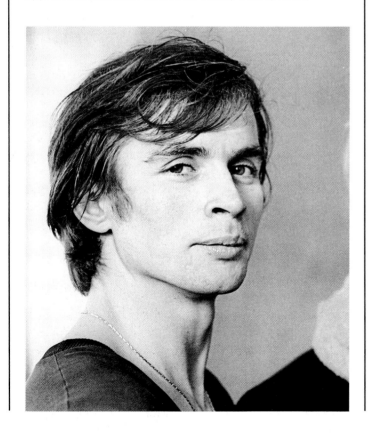

slowly, the most difficult of all technical feats, requiring the strength and control to sustain a *legato* through acrobatic contortions. But he can move fast when he wants to. He will change into 'overdrive' and assume an astonishing velocity in the final *manège* of a long solo. His beats are clear and strong, his pirouettes are done with a force which sometimes pushes them off balance: they are not just decorative spins but an expression of dynamics as forceful as a jump. He rarely 'cheats' in his *tours en l'air* but insists on a correct take-off and a landing in proper fifth position. He combines intensity of feeling with integrity of technique. Though it is laced with oriental softness. His dancing is essentially positive and masculine: he has not Nijinsky's androgynous ambiguity. But the effect he makes can be double-edged, with a sexual magnetism which is discernible by both men and women. This quality is backed by a presence of almost hypnotic force. When he walks on stage he seems able to switch on some inner dynamo that makes him glow with an invisible incandescence. This may be unconscious, but it is part of his professional achievement. He has a huge ego and he can, and does, harness it all to his dancing.

His range has proved remarkable, stretching from the proudest of Princes or the dreamy poet of *Les Sylphides*, to the romantic ardour of Romeo or the fiery authority of Apollo, from the mischief and comedy of the barber in *Don Quixote* to modern-style plasticity in works by Graham or Tetley. He searches continually for a choreographer who will add one more dimension to his protean dancing personality. A balletic ice-breaker, he is fortunately equipped with a sturdy engine and a psychological armour tough enough to withstand the pressures. In addition he has proved a fertile producer, devising highly individual versions of the old classics with a distinctive choreographic style, besides several original ballets; and in 1983 he took up his appointment as Director of ballet at the Paris Opéra. He has also made successful excursions into directing dance films, and has embarked on a subsidiary career as an actor in the cinema.

These varied and creative achievements reflect a character burning with curiosity, energy and adventure, in which an almost academic professionalism (he is a much valued coach), is always imbued with passion. He has been self-propelled and self-sufficient all his life, a lone ranger of the dance. A constellation rather than a star, he has excelled in many fields. To each he brings the whole of himself, and it is that self which has made him a legend.

VLADIMIR VASILIEV

n the context of Soviet ballet, Vasiliev's career is extraordinary. He graduated into the Bolshoi Ballet in 1958, at exactly the same time as Nureyev and Yuri Soloviev joined the Kirov. Any one of those would have been a matter for pride and congratulation; for one country to produce three such, simultaneously, seems almost incredible. Yet Nureyev was driven within three years to emigrate, and Soloviev some time later to suicide. Vasiliev alone remains – and remains in some triumph, with the title Honoured Artist and a Lenin Prize – remains, moreover, in spite of having been prepared to criticize the

Opposite, as Spartacus leading the revolt of the slaves in Yuri Grigorovich's production for the Bolshoi Ballet.

Below, as Danila, hero of *The Stone Flower*, with Nina Timofeyeva as the magical Mistress of the Copper Mountain.

artistic policies of the Bolshoi; of trying to introduce new and, by Russian ideas, revolutionary influences; and of bluntly declaring an admiration not only for older dancers who had remained in Russia, but also for Nureyev and Baryshnikov after their departure. Only a brave and gifted man could do that and survive.

Son of a truck driver and a factory clerk, Vasiliev was born in Moscow and recommended to the Bolshoi School by the leader of a folk dance troupe he joined when he was seven. He loved dancing but found ballet technique difficult and at first did not exert himself at it, but worked desperately when at last interest seized him. As a student, he attracted attention for his playing of the deformed, lovesick, murderous Malatesta in *Francesca da Rimini*, and within two months of joining the company he began to have solos, including what seems the unlikely assignment (given his age, appearance and temperament) of partnering Ulanova in *Chopiniana (Les Sylphides)*. Before he was twenty, Vasiliev had danced leading roles in three major ballets: as the unshakeably heroic Danila in the Moscow premiere of Grigorovich's *The Stone Flower*; as the dashing Prince in Zakharov's *Cinderella*; and creating the part of Ivanushka in a new version by Alexander Radunsky of the old Russian classic, *The Humpbacked Horse* (1960). This last, with Plisetskaya as the Tsar-Maiden, was filmed in 1961 and, together with tours to the United States, France, Britain and many other countries, soon made Western audiences aware of his gifts. The fun he found in the character of Ivanushka was heightened by the contrast between his jolly, simple appearance, with round face and flaxen hair, and the prodigious virtuosity of his dancing.

Vasiliev's most celebrated creation, and the greatest example of the modern Soviet heroic style, came with Grigorovich's new production of *Spartacus* in 1968. Earlier versions of this ballet had failed (Vasiliev had played the small role of a slave in one of them), but this one was a tremendous success, above all for the opportunities offered by three of the leading parts: not only Vasiliev's playing of the title part, but that of his wife, Ekaterina Maximova, as the heroine Phrygia, and Maris Liepa as the bold, weak but successfully opportunistic Roman leader Crassus. Part of the strength of Vasiliev's performance came from the sheer bravado and physical determination with which he hurled himself into his rousing solos, but he gave the character an almost messianic zeal, and brought out to the full the tragedy as

the revolt he led was overcome by force of numbers and superior arms.

Vasiliev insisted on trying to find a dramatic complexity within the characters he played; for instance, in Grigorovich's ballet *Ivan the Terrible*, emphasizing the high intentions with which Ivan started before circumstances turned him into a tyrant. Vasiliev was helped in the preparation of that role by Ulanova, just as he had earlier been helped by the coaching of two outstanding men of the older generation, his chief teacher, Mikhail Gabovich, and Alexei Yermolayev. In particular, Yermolayev worked with him on the ballet *Don Quixote*, devising more and more brilliant combinations of virtuoso steps for his solos, which Baryshnikov has remarked would have been inconceivable earlier. As Basilio, the mischievous hero of that ballet, Vasiliev achieved a soaring style which made the most difficult bravura passages look almost easy.

Vasiliev himself began choreography with an imaginative two-act *Icarus*, created in 1971 and revised five years later. The ballet had serious weaknesses, not least in its score and in the structure of its plot, but it succeeded in its main aim of representing a man of the heroic sort, the sort

Left, as Spartacus with his wife,
Ekaterina Maximova, as Phrygia.

Opposite, with Maximova in *The Nutcracker.*

that 'cause a disturbance, who bring an upheaval into the consciousness of those about them'. Even more impressive than Vasiliev's own lithe athleticism in suggesting flight with bold leaps around the stage, was the way he indicated the hero's desire to fly simply by the pose and angle of his balances, the stretch and thrust of his arms.

He was always conscious of the importance of expression as well as virtuosity, and pointed out that even a simple step of the classical vocabulary, for instance a jeté, can be made to express anything: despair or joy, drama, romance or lyricism. Also, he tried to draw on the experience of one role to throw fresh light on another, using as an example the fact that he derived far more understanding of the role of Albrecht in *Giselle* after he had danced *Spartacus*.

A role he danced early in his career was *Petrushka*, in a conventional staging by Boyarsky; then in 1977 he showed his adventurousness by appearing in a completely new version of the ballet created for him by Béjart. It required immense stamina: even before Petrushka makes his first appearance in the Fokine ballet, the hero of the new staging has already danced several solos and a duet; later he has to take on the music written for the Moor and the Ballerina as well as for the title role. More demandingly still, assuming multiple guises compelled the dancer to express the femininity and the brutality of those characters as well as his own nature. Yet the most impressive moment in Vasiliev's performance came at the end, when he simply walked somnambulistically through the crowds, puzzled and lonely, finally being left alone on the darkening stage with a spotlight lighting only his face until the last ironic bar of the music. In that moment, the quality that had illuminated all Vasiliev's roles became most vividly apparent: the gift of a warm and generous humanity inspiring all his actions.

ANTHONY DOWELL

Light, swift and elegant, Anthony Dowell is the embodiment of the Royal Ballet's English style. He took a long time to show his full potential, only comparatively recently breaking through his natural reserve to express the emotions needed for the great classical roles for which he is now justly famous. It was, however, in a classical solo that he first attracted attention, in Erik Bruhn's new production of dances from *Napoli*. Dowell was only nineteen at the time and had been in the company for just a year; since then he has danced all the classic leads but, more rewardingly, his sympathetic temperament and immaculate dancing have attracted many choreographers to create an unusually large number of roles especially for him, which have developed varied aspects of his gifts.

Frederick Ashton was the first to make a leading role for Dowell in 1964, as Oberon in *The Dream*, which also began his celebrated partnership with the slightly older Antoinette Sibley, by then already marked out as a ballerina in the making. Dowell's ability to give a neat, crisp quality to intricate combinations of steps encouraged Ashton to compose particularly brilliant solos for him, in *The Dream* and later in *Enigma Variations* (in which Dowell's bravura solo is almost explosive in its brusqueness). But if Ashton's *The Dream* woke Dowell to physical virtuosity, Antony Tudor's *Shadowplay* (1967) gave Dowell what he described as 'the shock of being taught to use my mind for the first time. Total concentration – I used that from then on'. In the allegory of a boy growing up, Tudor revealed both a fragile uncertainty and an inner strength in Dowell.

In *Manon* (1974) Kenneth MacMillan cast Dowell as Des Grieux, who grows from an almost naïve innocence to tempestuous passion, but it was Dowell himself who later asked to exchange roles at some performances with David Wall so that he could play Lescaut, the heroine's scheming brother, because he wanted a violent change; as he said, 'suddenly to be really evil and nasty was very exciting, riveting to do'. Although it was a world away from his usual roles as a fairy-tale prince or a romantic lover, the actual projection of the character – though not the character itself – corresponded to a firm, sharp quality in Dowell's nature. Although often praised for the smoothness of his dancing, Dowell never falls into blandness; his dancing always has an edge to it.

When Hans van Manen created *Four Schumann Pieces* for Dowell in 1975, he set out to reveal qualities hidden by his usual roles, putting in some deliberately unsmooth touches, and allowing the dancer to show a more brooding manner, both when motionlessly watching the ensemble, and in relationship to two women and another man in the dramatic adagio. Another neglected quality in Dowell appeared when he danced in Jerome Robbins' *Dances at a Gathering*: a sense of humour that made his two-man competitive duet with Nureyev even more amusing than exhilarating.

For years, it seemed that Dowell's career would exemplify the virtues of a permanent connection with one company and of a continuing partnership with one ballerina. The arrival of Natalia Makarova as guest with the Royal Ballet demonstrated that, harmonious as Dowell's partnership with Sibley had proved, setting him against a dancer of different temperament could spark a new, unexpected response in him. Similarly, when Dowell decided to spend a whole year dancing with American Ballet Theatre in 1979 (and subsequently has spent only part of each year with the Royal Ballet in order to accept

Opposite, Dowell with Antoinette Sibley in the *Meditation from 'Thaïs'* made for them by Frederick Ashton.

Below, with Lynn Seymour in the Royal Ballet's studios; the photograph behind them is of Brian Shaw.

Left, as Oberon in *The Dream*, which in 1964 was the first role created by Ashton for Dowell. It used his speed, and smooth but sharp quality of movement to present a dazzling and commanding character, and also laid the foundation of his long partnership with Sibley, who played Titania.

Right, Dowell dances Daphnis' solo in the first scene of Ashton's *Daphnis and Chloë*. He took the role after several other men had danced it, but the smooth classical elegance of Dowell's style brought out the quality of the ballet more clearly than it had been shown before, making this ardently poetic solo, in particular, a vivid expression of half-awakened innocent young love.

Right, as Des Grieux, the romantic hero of *Manon*, created for Dowell (with Sibley in the title role) by Kenneth MacMillan. Later, when Seymour played Manon, Dowell and Wall began to exchange roles at some performances, so that Dowell also played the unscrupulous anti-hero.

guest engagements elsewhere), it enabled him to develop a deeper sensibility, giving his dancing a firmer quality. His natural shyness, which had always made it difficult for him to portray romantic lovers, has given way to a new relaxation and maturity.

It was in America that Dowell experimented with diversification. He showed that he could speak lines effectively as the narrator in Ashton's Gertrude Stein ballet *A Wedding Bouquet*, and later in Stravinsky's *Oedipus Rex*. Another role in *Wedding Bouquet*, the dancing lead as the Bridegroom, enabled him to reveal a growing gift for comedy. Success and the interest of choreographers allowed Dowell to break the confines of the pure, princely style to which his physical gifts and reserved temperament might otherwise have condemned him. Like other outstanding male dancers, for Dowell the avoidance of stereotypes has been more rewarding for both himself and his audience.

RICHARD CRAGUN

Summon up a vision of Richard Cragun dancing, and the likelihood is that it will be of his Petruchio in *The Taming of the Shrew*, and probably one particular solo among many. It occurs at his wedding to Kate and shows at its best the breath-taking flight of Cragun's big, strongly-muscled body high above the stage, hurtling and swirling in great leaps that nobody else has ever quite been able to match. It is not just a matter of virtuoso tricks, such as his triple *tours en l'air*, but rather of the sheer flamboyant showmanship with which the bravura steps are presented.

It was seeing Gene Kelly and Donald O'Connor in film musicals that inspired the schoolboy Richard Cragun, in Sacramento, California, with a wish to dance like them; and his dancing has never lost the brash vigour he emulated in those hoofers. When he first started dancing classes, his teacher warned him that musicals demanded a wide range of techniques; so he tackled everything in the syllabus: baton twirling, dancing on roller skates, ballroom exhibition dancing, acrobatics – and even ballet. But he did not come to realize the theatrical possibilities of ballet until he saw a performance by the Royal Ballet on tour in California.

What fired his imagination was the sight of Alexander Grant, a superb Character dancer, as the sea-god Tirrenio in Ashton's *Ondine*. It gave him a new ambition, and he readily accepted Grant's advice to study at the Royal Ballet School, talking his family into letting him set off alone for distant England aged sixteen. He graduated after two years, in 1962, and immediately joined the Stuttgart Ballet, where a young new director, John Cranko, was building up the company to higher standards.

Cragun had no intention of staying any longer than it took him to save enough money for further studies in Russia. (Russian training would undoubtedly have suited his big, powerful physique, enabling him to specialize in roles of a Heroic nature.) But Cragun fell under Cranko's spell, and never left. His strength and extrovert personality would have ensured him a successful career anywhere, but Cranko made an international star of him. Like his Stuttgart contemporaries, Cragun is an example of what an imaginative choreographer-director can do to extend his dancers' range.

Although he won promotion to principal dancer by the age of twenty, Cragun's first roles were either secondary ones in big productions or leads in smaller works. But with both Cranko and Kenneth MacMillan mounting many ballets, new opportunities soon arose. His big chance came when the leading man, Ray Barra, was injured and retired early; Cragun at once moved from a supporting role in MacMillan's *Song of the Earth* to the long, heroic central part.

Cranko first brought Cragun to prominence in *Opus 1* in 1965, a ballet encapsulating a man's life and death in semi-abstract form. Believing that a dancer's job was to move, Cragun found it hard to accept that for part of the time he simply had to stand still, but when he sensed the serenity of that moment and began trying to convey it to the audience, he learned a valuable lesson in projection, one which he has continued to develop.

Another factor that helped to bring out his latent gifts was the chance to dance regularly with Marcia Haydée, a great dance-actress whose complete identification with every character she played inspired her partners to extend their own acting skills. And the repertory system at Stuttgart encouraged versatility; Cragun was given opportunities for instance, to alternate the roles of Mercutio and Romeo. But for a long time Cragun's strongest gifts remained his vigour, power and robust humour; they found their supreme revelation in Cranko's *The Taming of the Shrew* (1969).

That ballet, created for Cragun and Haydée, utilized his fine abilities as a partner to the full, since its duets included much literally knockabout comedy in which both dancers often ended flat on their backsides. Yet beneath the farcical encounters the dancers succeeded in conveying grudging admiration, growing affection and eventual tenderness.

Cragun made his New York debut in the *Shrew*, winning cheers from the audience. Other successes followed: Margot Fonteyn chose him to partner her in *Swan Lake*, and after Cranko's death in 1973, Glen Tetley provided major roles for Cragun at Stuttgart – as the athletically endowed victim in *The Rite of Spring*, and the mourning hero in *Voluntaries*.

Even when cast in romantic roles (as Eugene Onegin in Cranko's ballet, for instance, or the despairing lover in John Neumeier's *Lady of the Camellias*), Cragun tends to bring out the ebullient, extrovert side of the characters rather than their contemplative or introspective aspects. But within his range he has witty subtlety, for instance as

Wedding guests watch with amazement Cragun's wild and whirling leaps as Petruchio in The Taming of the Shrew.

Above, with Marcia Haydée as Kate in *The Taming of the Shrew*. | Right, thrown aloft as the chosen victim in Tetley's *Rite of Spring*.

the umbrella-carrying embodiment of British imperturbability in Cranko's *Brouillards*. Guest appearances with American Ballet Theatre brought him the chance to tackle Jerome Robbins's comic *Fancy Free*, with its overtones of the musicals he had enjoyed as a boy, and to play an unscrupulous seducer in Antony Tudor's *Pillar of Fire*.

With increasing maturity, he is turning to a different range of roles, as a singer might turn from baritone to bass. The young American choreographer William Forsythe

recognized and used a growing emotional depth in Cragun when he cast him as the tormented central figure in a two-act modern *Orpheus* (1979) at the time of a crisis in Cragun's own private life. Maurice Béjart, too, developed his gifts in a revised version of the unusual *Petrushka* originally made for Vasiliev. Though his most distinctive achievements have been in the robust virtuoso roles, there could be further developments still to come in Cragun's oeuvre.

PETER MARTINS

In the Royal Danish Ballet where he was trained and began his career, Peter Martins was seen as the tall, fair type of the Nordic classical dancer though he had a stubborn, independent nature which almost got him expelled from the school; fortunately his natural gifts were enough for his most influential teacher, Stanley Williams, to be able to save him.

Martins felt stifled in small-town Copenhagen and amid the company's rigid traditions. Although promoted aged twenty-one to a principal dancer, he was discontented and went one Saturday night in 1967 to ask Williams (by then teaching at the School of American Ballet) about the prospects of working in America. That very evening he was telephoned to go at once to Edinburgh where a small group of New York City Ballet dancers was appearing and needed a replacement for an injured dancer in *Apollo*. Martins knew the role and none of the more famous Apollos was available. His success led to guest appearances with New York City Ballet in their home theatre and, after a couple of years, to the decision to move permanently to New York.

That opportunity with *Apollo* was the second important stroke of luck in Martins' career. The first was when he accompanied his sisters to their audition at the Royal Danish Ballet School and was accepted, though they were not. Apart from that, he has made his own way, sometimes painfully. On joining Balanchine's New York company he found the adjustment physically and intellectually difficult. His big body had problems with the choreographic demands; his European formality and aim for 'correctness' (on stage and off) seemed, in his own word, 'prissy'; and he could not understand the purpose behind Balanchine's classes which, by most standards, were eccentric – being intended for his own choreographic purposes. Martins even got to the point of having a contract prepared to join the rival company, American Ballet Theatre, with its more traditional repertory where he would have been a star in the standard classics. But an instinct pushed him back to Balanchine and the two men began to understand each other.

It was actually in Robbins' ballets that Martins began to feel at home: with created roles in *In The Night* (1970) and *Goldberg Variations* (1971). The first role Balanchine created on him was the Stravinsky *Violin Concerto* (1972); in it Martins began to appreciate Balanchine's concern for the quality of movement, for contrasts, breaking down patterns and building new ones. In

working on this and *Duo Concertant* for the Stravinsky Festival of 1972, Martins wrote that Balanchine made him 'discover how I could vary, extend and increase the range of the way I danced . . . He made me give up . . . any fear of looking inadequate or awkward . . . What he was allowing me to discover was my own way of moving.' In this work he found a way of using his naturally large movements with subtle delicacy.

With that discovery, Martins was able to grow into one of the 'stars' of a company whose avowed policy was to have no stars. Martins proved to be an exceptional

Martins, below, as Apollo, the role that brought about his association with Balanchine and New York City Ballet when he played it at short notice in an emergency.

A link, right, between Martins' Danish origins and his main career in New York: in the solo from *Flower Festival at Genzano* in the Bournonville divertissement produced for New York City Ballet by his old teacher Stanley Williams.

dancing partner with great skill at showing off a ballerina to her best advantage in a way that enhanced the effect of what both of them were contributing to the ballet. He was often put to partner Suzanne Farrell (whose first comment on meeting him before their short-notice *Apollo* in Edinburgh, had been 'At least he's tall'). Their mutual adventurousness in exploring the possibilities of Balanchine's choreography created an excitement on stage that gave their performances together a keen following.

Yet Martins' ambitions changed as he grew more at home in the company. At one time, he admits, he had wanted to be 'the best dancer in the world', and yet he often felt uncomfortable before an audience. He came to terms with his size, and learned that he must use his height and bulk to make his dancing 'read large' and clear, using his body and limbs to the full. He also had the idea that 'personality' was not a matter of being outrageous or uninhibited, but of being self-aware, 'having your own opinions which you were secure enough about that you didn't have to advertise yourself'.

His appearance changed, and from being almost conventionally beautiful as a young man he developed more distinctive, leonine good looks, and his whole style took on an independence, emphasis and focus which enabled him to present the almost always non-narrative, music-based choreography of Balanchine and Robbins in a way that gave pleasure to an audience not by any ingratiating qualities, but simply by showing his own understanding of it as clearly and fully as possible. In so doing, he helped develop further the distinctively American classical style evolved by dancers like Villella, Jacques d'Amboise and other native-born Americans with whom he worked. Martins began to play a more conscious part in that process when he turned to choreography, in the late seventies, and found that he enjoyed watching other dancers' bodies in rehearsal more than his own in the studio mirror.

From then, he limited his own stage appearances. His new activity enabled him, on Balanchine's death in 1983, to take over responsibility for New York City Ballet's direction, jointly with Robbins. Unfortunately that has necessitated his withdrawal from the stage to concentrate on teaching, choreographing and other directorial responsibilities. However, in a career that has been individual, allowing him to find his own powerful, grainy version of classic style, Martins' greatest influence in the evolution of male dancing could be only now beginning.

Below, a Character role as the sensuous occupant of a sunny dance studio in Robbins' *Afternoon of a Faun*.

Opposite, three aspects of his celebrated partnership with Suzanne Farrell, all in ballets by Balanchine: top left, lyrical in *Chaconne* to the ballet music from Gluck's *Orpheus*; top right, brilliantly classical in *Diamonds* to most of Tchaikovsky's Third Symphony; below, expressively neo-classical in the Stravinsky *Apollo*.

MIKHAIL BARYSHNIKOV

The special interest of Baryshnikov's dancing arises partly from an individual collection of contradictory qualities. He has the natural style, fluency and serenity of the pure *danseur noble* within a body that, although well-proportioned, is compact (as a student, he was disturbed at being the shortest boy in his class), and would seem to indicate a demi-caractère type. Although his physical facility in the academic technique makes him unrivalled in his day as an exponent of classic virtuosity, his temperament leads him towards experiment and new experiences.

Born in Riga, capital of Latvia, Baryshnikov started dancing late – he was already twelve – but benefited from the outstanding ballet school there before moving to the Kirov School in Leningrad, where the great teacher Pushkin helped develop the youth's exceptional skill and personal style just as he had done earlier for Nureyev. Like Nureyev, Baryshnikov graduated into the Kirov Ballet as a soloist, but was cast chiefly according to his physical type: for instance, in the showpiece 'peasant pas de deux' rather than the romantic Albrecht in *Giselle*. His immense flair, attractive personality and blond, open good looks quickly made him a star, but he had to struggle and plot to get the few created roles that came his way. Frustrated by the lack of interesting choreographers and restricted repertory in Russia, he took the opportunity of a tour to Canada in 1974 to remain in the West.

He was twenty-six, and hunted eagerly for new experiences. Although his main attachment was to American Ballet Theatre, he appeared with many other companies and took on a range of roles, not all of high quality. However, he was able to appear in works by Balanchine and Antony Tudor, whose ballets he greatly admired, and had an immense success in a ballet unlike anything previously made for him, as the slick, wildly comic hero of Twyla Tharp's *Push Comes To Shove* (1976). His range grew as he tackled ballets by Ashton, MacMillan, Roland Petit and Paul Taylor, danced many of the old classics, and had party pieces made for him by Jerome Robbins, Alvin Ailey, Eliot Feld and others.

Like Nureyev, Baryshnikov had rapidly become as great a celebrity with the general public as with a dance audience, and that was reinforced when he starred, as both dancer and actor, in the film *The Turning Point* (1977), playing what was widely thought to be a semi-autobiographical part as the young Russian dancer who is irresistible romantically as well as professionally. But in 1978 Baryshnikov suddenly gave up everything else to join New York City Ballet without the special privileges and high earnings open to him everywhere else. This decision was made partly because he wanted to work with Balanchine, whom he thought the greatest choreographer of his day (and with whom he shared a Petersburg/Leningrad background); partly, also, because, as his New York City Ballet colleague Peter Martins wrote, he 'felt uneasy with his success, and yearned for the kind of structure that he had had as a member of the Kirov'. He stayed there for two years and danced many ballets by Balanchine and Robbins, adapting more quickly than most newcomers to the different stylistic emphasis, but eventually beginning to worry that concentration on these works was making him lose some of his technical mastery in other modes. An invitation to succeed Lucia Chase, one of American Ballet Theatre's founders, as director of the company proved to be the challenge that took him back there in 1980.

The new responsibilities caused him to restrict his own stage appearances, but he remained ABT's most popular star and still undertook some guest performances, notably with the Royal Ballet. His presence there stimulated

Right, Baryshnikov in the mock-heroic *Variations on 'America'* made for him by Eliot Feld to Charles Ives' music.

Opposite, bottom right, Baryshnikov in one of Balanchine's most individual ballets, *Four Temperaments*.

Opposite, top, Baryshnikov in another famous Balanchine role, the title part in *The Prodigal Son*.

Opposite, bottom left, in *Pas de 'Duke'*, created for him by Alvin Ailey to music by Duke Ellington.

Above, with Natalia Makarova in *Other Dances*, created for them by Jerome Robbins to Chopin's piano music.

Left, Baryshnikov in a solo by Erik Bruhn for Siegfried in *Swan Lake*, which he danced with the Royal Ballet.

Above, Baryshnikov in exuberant mood as Romeo in the Royal Ballet's production of *Romeo and Juliet*.

Ashton to create *Rhapsody*, his most substantial ballet for several years, with a virtuoso central role based on Baryshnikov's speed and ability to produce explosive brilliance within a smooth continuity. As Peter Martins wrote, Baryshnikov was the 'only dancer who didn't make you focus on the trick itself, for he managed to incorporate the trick into the role. This ability came from his sense of style, his stage sense. He was always tasteful, never tacky, and this abetted his phenomenal physical ability.'

Perhaps because of his apparently easy mastery of technical virtuosity, Baryshnikov seems not to have the overwhelming commitment to dancing that some of his contemporaries reveal. There is a certain reticence of personality, certainly not of effort, in his dancing, and his private life is as important to him as his career. Yet he brings a serious purpose to his work, shown by his own comments and by the policies he adopted for Ballet Theatre. These emphasize style rather than showmanship, the collective effort rather than star appeal (even – perhaps especially – his own), and the vital importance of long-term policies.

Those qualities explain how he works, but they do not explain the phenomenon of his great talent. What the public sees when watching him dance is an exceptional skill put to expressive use to reveal the character of the role or, in a plotless work, the choreographic style. Also, and above all, it sees a man with a rare gift for conveying the joy of the dance itself, pure and undiluted.

JORGE DONN

At the age of sixteen, Jorge Donn was already obsessed by dance and appearing with the ballet company at the Teatro Colón in his native Buenos Aires. Had he stayed there, he might or might not have had a successful career, but could easily never have been heard of outside Argentina. His life changed when the Ballet of the Twentieth Century from Brussels arrived for a guest season. Bowled over by Maurice Béjart's work, Donn asked to be allowed to join. There was no vacancy, but later that year he managed to make his way to Brussels, where his evident enthusiasm, his promise and another dancer's temporary absence led to his acceptance.

In a sense, Donn's entire career since then has been as Béjart's pupil. There was a spell when he left for Paris with thoughts of becoming an actor; there have been guest appearances with New York City Ballet, the Bolshoi, the Stuttgart Ballet (in each case partnering a major ballerina, respectively Suzanne Farrell, Maya Plisetskaya and Marcia Haydée, with whom he had previously worked in Brussels). Donn, however, describes Béjart as not just his director and choreographer, not just his ideal teacher, but also as his guru. It was Béjart's insistence on bringing philosophy into dance that won Donn to his side, and Donn's unique greatness lies in being able to imply a philosophic content to the most physical of all arts.

A big, powerfully muscled man with a mane of golden hair, he seems meant by nature to be the archetype of the heroic dancer, but under Béjart's spell he can transform himself to the wicked angel of *Notre Faust* or the rock star in *Dichterliebe*. The phrase 'under a spell' seems literally true when Donn describes how, during the months of playing the mad and tragic central figure in *Nijinsky, Clown de Dieu*, he felt as though drugged, and actually suffered withdrawal symptoms when the run was over.

Béjart's worldwide success (with audiences, though not everywhere with critics) is based only partly on his ideas. He also relies to a large extent on an eye for visual effect and a sense of physical excitement: it is significant that he finds ballet, as an art form, closely connected with cinema and with sport. A very strict and academic teacher of ballet technique himself, he insists on teachers of the highest quality for his company, and that technique is the basis of their work, however much oriental or popular influence is added. In addition, he believes in nurturing dancers, as a gardener grows plants, tending them with individual loving care.

Above, as Nijinsky in Béjart's fantasy treatment of his life and work, *Nijinsky, Clown de Dieu*.

Right, as Icarus, one of his roles in another of Béjart's epics, *Nôtre Faust*.

Donn benefited from all this, and from Béjart's emphasis on male dancing at the expense of all but a few of the women in his company. But what has made him the greatest of the many exceptional male dancers to emerge from the Béjart company are two qualities: the compelling force of his personality and the absolutely single-minded dedication of his work. If he has a life outside the dance, it is a well-kept secret; he has even said that he does not go to other performances, or other cultural events, because 'I feel that today people are entirely too well informed about things'. In class, he looks ordinary. It is on stage that his charisma emerges, transforming, for instance, his dancing of the title part in Béjart's *Firebird* into an incarnation of revolutionary fervour; or to convert his nearly naked body, driving itself to exhaustion on a huge table-top in *Bolero*, into a potent image of sexual desire, aureoled by the sweat that flings away from him as he spins in a spotlight.

Below, on a table-top surrounded by the corps de ballet in the all-male version of Béjart's Ravel *Bolero*.

Peter Schaufuss

At his graduation performance as an aspirant with the Royal Danish Ballet, Peter Schaufuss could already show the potential of his airborne virtuosity in his solo from the second act of *Giselle*. It was this role which won him ovations when he danced it a decade later at the Metropolitan Opera House, New York, partnering Makarova, as a guest with American Ballet Theatre. But during the intervening years his career often looked as though it had gone seriously wrong.

His parents were both dancers. His father, Frank Schaufuss, had partnered Fonteyn and had directed the Royal Danish Ballet for a time. His mother, Mona Vangsaae, was a Bournonville ballerina of a style and delicacy not seen since her generation retired. Through their influence Peter Schaufuss reached a technical peak while still a teenager, but partly perhaps because of some misplaced parental advice he took some time to settle the course of his subsequent career. He danced in Canada, returned to Denmark, left again for an engagement with London Festival Ballet (making his debut in their *Sleeping Beauty*, a major classic he had never even seen before), made guest appearances with many minor companies, then joined New York City Ballet. However a serious back condition incapacitated him for almost a year before he could begin to make his mark there.

Doctors and surgeons in New York told him he would never dance again, but he found an osteopath in London prepared to treat him. That traumatic period forced Schaufuss to reassess his character and attitude to life and work, as well as to his body. When he began dancing again, it was with a changed temperament and an enhanced virtuosity, shown for instance in the speed and fire he brought to Balanchine's *Rubies* (a role in which he stood up to comparison with Villella and Baryshnikov).

Following an unexpected *Giselle* with Makarova (the result of an injury to her usual partner), he also decided that romantic and dramatic ballets suited him better than New York City Ballet's repertory. Thereafter he took an engagement as a principal with the National Ballet of Canada as his base, while stepping up his guest engagements, which enabled him to work with choreographers such as Roland Petit and Kenneth MacMillan, and to perform with the Royal Ballet and the Ballet of the Paris Opéra, among others.

A solo for a gala to show off Schaufuss' spectacular elevation and virile manner.

Left, a beautifully poised attitude displaying the pure Classical style.

Above, the exuberance of the romantic Bournonville style as James in *La Sylphide*.

Schaufuss can tackle a range of roles from the sinister hero of Petit's *Phantom of the Opera* to the sheer virtuosity of Harald Lander's *Etudes*. With his Danish background, he has made a speciality of Bournonville's classics (himself mounting *La Sylphide* and *Napoli* to much acclaim), although he approaches them with a deliberate broadening of their effects and techniques which he thinks necessary for modern audiences and theatres. His dancing has a dare-devil recklessness, in the way he tackles the standard solos as well as in the breath-taking new tricks which, like one or two other virtuoso dancers (Baryshnikov the most prominent), he invents to embellish his work.

Yet at heart, he knows that character means more than tricks. Although his sturdy build and powerfully devel-oped muscles enable him to stun an audience with dazzling feats, they can be only the highlight of a performance, and even in a showpiece like the *Corsaire* pas de deux he follows Nureyev's example of investing the steps with meaning as well as brilliance. In Ashton's *La Fille mal gardée* he plays not only the romantic hero Colas but also his comic, silly rival Alain, alternating the two parts at different performances to let audiences see his versatility. In technical and material resources, Schaufuss has travelled far beyond Bournonville, his Danish prede-cessor of a century or more earlier, but he retains the same spirit. His greatest desire has been to use the full range of dance skill as a form of drama, and to give pleasure to an audience by conveying to them something of his own *joie de vivre*.